AF372716

K. J. Adcock

Leather: From the Raw Material to the Finished Product

e-artnow 2024

K. J. Adcock

Leather: From the Raw Material to the Finished Product

e-artnow, 2024
Contact: eartnow.info@gmail.com

ISBN: 978-80-273-8900-1

Contents

CHAPTER I EVOLUTION OF THE ART OF LEATHER MANUFACTURE

Before describing the making of leather by up-to-date methods, it may be useful to attempt to outline the evolution of the ancient art of tanning and dyeing skins. As everyone knows, leather is the preserved skin of various animals, but the origin of the conversion of raw skins into an imputrescible material will probably never be traced, and it can only be assumed that the processes necessary to produce leather from skins were gradually and, in most cases, accidentally discovered. Long before the Christian era, the ancient Egyptians had succeeded in bringing the manufacture of leather to remarkable perfection, and, had they at their service the wonderful machinery now available to the leather industry, it is certain that their productions would have lost little or nothing by comparison with modern leather. Happily, specimens of ancient Egyptian leather have been preserved in one national museum, and, although they are said to have been made at least 3,000 years ago, the colour and natural strength of the leather are unimpaired.

Judging by the advanced state of the art of leather manufacture in the early Egyptian period, it is obvious that the origin of its manufacture must have considerably antedated that period, and, indeed, it would be necessary to go back almost to the creation of man to find the origin of the use of preserved animal skins for clothing. The primitive method would naturally consist of simply drying the skin, in which condition it would keep for many years unless it came into contact with moisture, though its horniness would no doubt cause the wearer much discomfort. It must not be supposed that the wearing of dried raw skins with the hair left on was impracticable, for even to-day some of the skins of fur-bearing animals used for personal adornment are cured in this primitive way, with the additional treatment with napthalene for disinfecting purposes and keeping away injurious insects and moths, the object of the limited amount of dressing being to preserve the natural strength and coloration of the fur. In such a condition, however, the skins are liable to acquire an unpleasant odour, and for hygienic reasons it is advisable that all skins in the hair used for clothing or rugs should be properly dressed, so that no decay sets in to loosen the hair or fur.

Even now, the process of simply drying hides and skins to preserve them before sending them to the tanner is largely practised, especially in hot climates and in those countries where salt is not readily available. This process of curing rests on the chemical theory of dehydration, which, in a modified form, has recently been successfully applied to some experiments in making leather.

Finding that the simple drying of skins would not properly prepare them for clothing, primeval man would naturally look for some means of treating them to conserve their original softness and pliability, and the nearest substances at hand would be animal fats and brains. It is almost safe to assume that this process was the first by which hides were preserved in a state differing from their original condition, the oxidation of the fatty matters naturally producing a partial tannage. The effect of smoke may also have been discovered in the earliest days of skin-curing, and it is reported that even now one or two tribes use smoke to preserve skins.

The somewhat imperfect preservation of the hides by this method would lead to further experiments being made, which evidently resulted in the discovery of the tanning effect of leaves, twigs, and barks of trees when soaked in water. It may be that the preservative effect of alum was discovered even before the vegetable tanning process, for the original Japanese white leather was made simply by steeping the raw hides in certain rivers which contained a bed-rock of alum. This primitive process is even followed to-day in one or two places in Japan, but the leather is afterwards treated with oil to impart tensile strength and increased suppleness. Strictly speaking, these hides are not leather when finished, and they are quite unsuitable for boots; but, being the toughest material known in the leather trade, with the possible exception of raw hide, it is particularly suitable and chiefly used for brace ends, and occasionally for ladies' belts. It must not be inferred from reference to this process that the Japanese only use this earliest method of making leather; on the contrary, they are producing all classes of leather, and especially belting and sole, by modern European methods, and it may not be long before their competition with American and European productions becomes an accomplished fact.

The available information seems to show that, until about thirty years ago, the development of the industry was mainly the result of accidental discoveries, and that the theory of tanning and leather-dressing was imperfectly understood until within quite recent times. Records of the leather trade 300 years ago prove that the methods then in vogue were of the rudest kind; further, they show that the practice of skimping the tanning process was not unknown in those days, for a contemporaneous author describes the horny condition of some of the leather which, despite the Government inspection, appeared to have passed into the old Leadenhall market for sale by the simple operation of "greasing the fist of the seller." Spain and Hungary had by that time established the manufacture of morocco and curried leather on a fairly sound basis, while a few years later France began to develop the industry of leather manufacture. Until about twenty years ago, waxed calf, crup, calf kid, and alum-tanned kid were staple upper leathers, together with the old Spanish cordovan leather. The sole leather used in England was chiefly the output of tanneries in the United Kingdom. About twenty years ago, however, the successful application of the chrome tanning process caused quite a revolution in the leather trade, with the result that about nine-tenths of the world's production of boot upper leather is chrome-tanned. The introduction of this process on a practical scale gave a great impetus to the work of chemists, who have since made some remarkable discoveries and have placed the art of leather manufacture on a scientific basis.

The old methods, however, are by no means obsolete, and it is somewhat remarkable to find that a British patent was taken out last year (1914) for converting hides and skins into leather by treating them with brains and smoke.

CHAPTER II HIDES AND SKINS

The hides and skins of animals form the principal raw material of the tanner. Technically, the term "hides" is applied to the skins of the larger animals, while the word "skins" is used in the case of the smaller animals. Thus, the tanner speaks of ox, cow, bull and horse *hides*, and of calf, sheep, and goat *skins*. There is an intermediate size between a full-grown calf skin and a small hide, and this is known as a "kip," but the line of demarcation is not very clear.

Buyers often settle the difficulty by examining the growth marks and the irregular substance of the skin, and, if these are marked features, it is classified as a kip. The condition of the hides of cattle is usually inferior during the six months after the animal has become a yearling. East India tanned hides, which are largely imported into England, are frequently described as E.I. "kips" in the trade. This is hardly accurate, but the mistake is probably due to the small size of full-grown Indian hides, which are very little larger than the average European kips. It is interesting to observe that furriers always refer to both their raw material and the finished product as skins, irrespective of the size of the fur-bearing animals. Most of the skins of wild animals are dressed without removing the hair or fur, and this is quite a distinct trade from leather manufacture, the only exception being the dressing of closely cut and fine-haired calf skins for slippers and fancy articles.

Practically every country in the world contributes to the supply of hides and skins, but there are a few countries which are far in advance of the others in the industries of cattle and sheep-raising. The sources of tanners' raw material have undergone great changes since the establishment of freezing and chilling stores for the preparation of meat for export, and the market prices of hides are to a large extent controlled by the supply in North and South America, South Africa, and Australia. Whether or not the concentration of these huge meat works into two or three centres is likely to benefit the leather trade is a debatable point. The flaying, trimming, and curing of hides in these establishments are certainly superior to the work done by the average butcher, while, owing to the large numbers of cattle slaughtered, the hides can be closely selected. On the other hand, the value of hides and skins has risen enormously in the last decade, the period coincident with the rapid growth of the chilled and frozen meat industry, but the increased use of leather in many directions may be mainly responsible for the higher cost of the raw material, although it is obvious that the concentration of the chief supplies of hides in a few lands must tend to increase the severity of the competition among buyers. Apart from the high prices of the hides, the concentration of the meat industry in large chilling and freezing works has had the effect of increasing the prices of beef and mutton, which are now higher in price than freshly-killed English meat was a few years ago. It appears to have been a grave error on the part of the British Government when they stopped the imports of live cattle owing to the fear of foot-and-mouth disease being communicated to domestic herds. The disease has broken out in several places since the embargo was imposed, so that the theory that the infection was only carried by imported live cattle has been clearly disproved. The butchering of cattle provides a large amount of work in subsidiary industries, and the Government embargo on the importation of live cattle has caused a great deal of distress in Deptford and Birkenhead, where large abattoirs were erected for the reception of live cattle, which used to be imported in fairly large numbers. There is no danger of foot-and-mouth disease getting beyond the abattoirs or of the slaughter of diseased cattle for food, and both tanners and butchers hope to see the removal of the embargo. So far as possible, each country should raise its own cattle to provide its own meat supply, and this principle is recognised by many countries which prohibit the import of foreign meat: but, owing to the rapid growth of populations in industrial countries, with the consequent increase in the value of land, it has become impracticable to raise enough cattle to supply domestic needs. Even the United States of America, which formerly had a great cattle-raising industry, has lately been obliged to import live cattle to meet the requirements of its inhabitants. Similar conditions prevail almost throughout Europe, and tanners have to look to South America, Australia, and Africa for large supplies of raw hides, although there are still some tanners in the United Kingdom who use only the hides produced in this country.

The bulk of the production of hides and skins in the United Kingdom is disposed of at weekly public auctions in the principal towns: London, Manchester, Liverpool, Leeds, Birmingham, Newcastle, and Glasgow being the largest centres of distribution. However, there is still a large quantity bought by private treaty, and opinions are divided as to which is the better method of buying. Before the establishment of public auctions, hides were very cheap, but tanners were unable to get a good selection, although, for sole leather, that was not a very important matter. Public auctions have become so firmly established that it would be impossible for tanners to revert to the old system even if they desired it. The competition of private buyers with the auction markets has certainly benefited the butcher at the expense of the tanner, and the weighing and classification of hides ultimately became so irregular in many markets that the Tanners' Federation of the United Kingdom had to take strong action not long ago to protect their interests. They demanded the appointment of an independent inspector at each market to check the weighing and sorting of the hides, but this was successfully resisted by the market proprietors, who eventually agreed to the tanners appointing travelling inspectors to visit the markets periodically. The system is said to have improved matters.

The English markets do not collect enough hides to permit their close sorting, so that, while the hides are graded according to weight and quality and the sex of the animal, the question of varying substances is generally ignored. There is usually a difference of 10 lb. in each class where the hides are sorted by weight Ox, cow, heifer, and bull hides are sold separately, as each sort has a different value. Bull hides are comparatively poor in quality, owing to their irregular substance and strong growth marks in the neck. Ox hides are the most suitable for sole leather and belting, while cows' and heifers' are used mainly for dressing hides, which are finished into bag, case, strap, and boot leathers. The hides known as Scotch and Hereford runts are the best of those produced in the United Kingdom, as they are well-grown, compact, and well-suited to the making of sole leather and belting. The grading of the weight of these hides at the auction markets is generally as follows: 100 lb. and above, 90-99 lb., 80-89 lb., 70-79 lb., 60-69 lb., 59 lb. and less. This does not give an ideal classification, as hides vary so much in texture and substance, and it is quite possible to find spready hides of poor substance and quality which would be heavier than a small but compact and well-grown hide. It would be better from the tanner's point of view if the hides were selected according to substance and quality. There are not many bull hides grown in the United Kingdom, and in many markets they are not classed by weight but simply into best and secondary qualities. Horse hides are of even less value than those of bulls, owing to their weaker texture and irregular substance. That part of the skin under the mane is almost worthless, while the flanks and sides are only useful for a secondary class of boot upper leather, although some fairly good patent sides have lately been produced from horse hide, which is suitable for that purpose owing to its soft grain and pliable texture when tanned. The most valuable part of a horse hide is the butt, which consists of the part known as the "shell." This shell is covered with an extremely fine grain which is not found in any other part of the hide. The well-known crup leather is made from the shell of the horse hide.

In addition to hides, there are fairly large quantities of calf and sheep skins sold at the weekly auctions, but veal is not such an important article of food in England as it is on the Continent. Sheep skins are far more numerous, as Great Britain is a big mutton-consuming country. Home supplies of both hides and skins have been greatly reduced, however, by the immense import of frozen and chilled meat.

Although the domestic supply of hides and skins is quite inadequate to meet the needs of British tanners, a large proportion is exported. American tanners buy large quantities of the best hides and pickled sheep skins. The latter are dewoolled and preserved by a process of pickling with formic or sulphuric acid and salt before exportation. Those preliminary operations are the work of the fellmonger. Nearly all of the horse hides produced in the United Kingdom are, or were before the War, sent to Germany, and British leather-dressers appear to have lost the art of finishing horse hide, or are unable to convert it into leather profitably.

The interchange of raw hides between various countries, and even between those where leather manufacture is an important industry, is somewhat remarkable, and only goes to prove that the concentration of a particular industry in one or two centres of the world gives these places a great advantage in regard to labour, organisation, and technical skill, even over those countries where the raw material is plentiful. Theoretically and economically it should be advantageous to establish tanneries close to the supply of raw hides, since the latter, under present conditions of preservation, steadily deteriorate from the time they are removed from the carcase until they reach the tannery. In some countries the methods of preserving hides are actually so bad that the hides have often lost half of their value before the tanner gets them. Two or three of the largest American meat-packing establishments have erected or taken over tanneries to deal with raw hides, one of their by-products. Tanneries have also been erected near some of the large meat works in the Argentine, but the development of the leather trade there is by no means rapid, and at present the United States of America is the largest leather-producing country in the world. Germany, France, and the United Kingdom come next in the order named.

South Africa is an important source of supply of raw material, and large quantities of Cape hides are sent to England. The production of raw hides there is likely to be on a very large scale in a few years' time, as the raising of Afrikander and other breeds of cattle is sure to become an important industry now that the ravages of the terrible disease, known as "tick," have been checked. China is another large hide-exporting country; most of the hides from this source are dried in the open air and are generally arsenicated to prevent the ravages of insects. Immense quantities are also provided in all other populous countries, but the demand for leather is generally greater than the production of raw material in those countries. India is a noteworthy exception to this general rule; the production of Indian hides is enormous, and, although the leather trade is being developed, there is a large surplus of raw hides and skins for export. Large quantities are roughly tanned, however, and exported to England, Germany, France, and other European countries to be dressed and finished. The greater proportion of these hides and skins is used for the making of shoe leather, while a good quantity is used for bag (hide) and imitation morocco (goat) leathers.

Naturally, there is in the aggregate a considerable supply of raw hides and skins from other parts of the world in addition to that from the countries specially named, and new sources are being frequently found.

It would be impossible to describe the characteristics of the numerous varieties of hides and skins except in a full-sized text-book, but a brief description of the principal sorts may be given.

Some of the varieties produced in the United Kingdom have already been described. In the main, there is not a great deal of difference in the hides of various breeds, but there is a type of well-grown and stout hides specially suitable for sole and belting leather; this class is known as runts, and these hides are obtained from the Scotch and Hereford breeds of cattle. The Scotch runts from the Highland cattle are more valuable than any other class of hide found in the United Kingdom; unfortunately, the production is small. Irish cattle also yield good hides, but in England the interests of the cattle owner, or feeder, are in conflict with those of the tanner, for the system of artificially fattening cattle with oil cakes tends to make the hides very greasy and weaker in the fibres than those hides from animals which are reared on natural food-stuffs.

This grease is very difficult to remove and reduces the selling value of sole leather by about 2d. per lb. The use of a borax solution for soaking partially removes the grease, while it has been proposed that the pelts should be treated with a solution of hyposulphite of soda just before placing them in the tan liquors. A drawback of the latter process is that a little weight is lost in the finished leather.

The trouble caused by the presence of a large quantity of natural grease is even more pronounced in sheep skins than in cattle hides. Naturally, a sheep arrives at maturity in about two years; but by the modern system of intensive feeding with oily food-stuffs it can be fattened in about ten months. This is obviously a great advantage to the sheep-breeder; in other respects it is an unsatisfactory method, for the mutton is not so well matured, and, therefore, is not so nourishing; it contains too large a proportion of fat, and the skins are very greasy and weak in fibre. The excess of grease does not detract from the value of the wool, and may even be beneficial.

There are several varieties of sheep in the United Kingdom, with widely different characteristics. A fellmonger should have a good knowledge of the skins of various breeds in order to buy the particular sorts that will meet the requirements of his customers, as his business is to separate the wool from the skins and to supply the former to the woollen factories and the latter to the leather-dressers. He has, therefore, to study carefully both the wool and pelt markets. While some breeds of sheep yield fine long wool of bright lustre, others have comparatively short-stapled, and "kempy" wool. Between these two classes, there are numerous grades, and the task of sorting the various qualities of wool in those fellmongeries where several classes of skins are worked is by no means easy. It is a generally accepted axiom that the pelt (*i.e.*, the skin denuded of wool) is weaker in fibre in those skins which yield the finest and best wool. In support of this, the Welsh mountain sheep may be cited. This sheep has short, curly wool, but its skin is tough and strong on the grain. In fact, it is about the only breed suitable for roller leather, which is used in the cotton industry for covering the drawing rollers of spinning-machines. Most of this leather is made in North Wales, whence it is exported to every country where the cotton industry is carried on.

Notable exceptions of the general rule regarding the relative qualities of wool and pelts are found in two or three English varieties, namely: the Lincolns, Leicesters and black-faced Suffolks, which produce both fine wool and large pelts of good quality.

Other useful British breeds are the Southdowns, Devons, Shropshires, Wensleydales, Scotch black-faced, Cotswolds, and Kerrys. Of the imported varieties, the New Zealand and Cape sheep skins are the best. The former, principally merino stock, not only provide very fine wool, but also pelts of choice quality and large pattern. Although the quality of the wool of Australian merino sheep is little, if any, inferior to that of the New Zealand type, the skins are not so good in quality, due, no doubt, to the hotter climate, which is favourable to the breeding of insects and other pests which damage the skins. The Cape sheep provide a skin which is quite different in texture from that of any other breed. It has a certain looseness of texture and softness of grain which make it particularly suitable for the manufacture of glove leather.

South America is another large sheep-breeding country; but the skins of this variety are not largely imported into England, most of them being sent to Mazamet, the great centre of the fellmongering industry in France. Buenos Aires skins are the most favoured of the South American skins, owing to their large size and good substance. Monte Videos are also very fine skins.

Smyrnas and Bagdads are other well-known varieties, but they are generally imported in a rough-tanned condition, or, as it is known technically, "in the crust." Leather-dressers finish them for various purposes, but mainly for boot and shoe lining leather. When properly tanned by the natives, these skins produce a supple finish, especially those of the Smyrna variety. Unfortunately, many lots are merely coloured on the surface with the tan liquor, with the result that they dry hard and tinny; such partially-tanned leather is very difficult to finish and is rarely satisfactory. Even when the tannage is completed elsewhere before finishing them, they never produce such good leather as skins properly tanned in the first instance.

Russia is another important country for the production of all kinds of raw hides and skins suitable for leather manufacture. American tanners buy very largely from this market, and a few enterprising firms even send their own representatives to the great annual fair held at Nishni Novgorod, where large quantities of dried hides and skins, besides many other kinds of produce, are offered for sale. British tanners take comparatively little interest in this important supply, but, as a result of the great European War, an increase of trade between Russia and the United

Kingdom is anticipated, although the Russian leather trade is developing rapidly and will absorb increasing quantities of native raw material.

Excepting a few in Ireland, raw goat skins are not produced in Great Britain. The chief drawback to goat breeding there is a somewhat inexplicable aversion on the part of the public to the flesh of goats; although another reason may be the destructive nature of the animals themselves, for they devour and uproot anything edible that comes in their way. It is, perhaps, unfortunate that some of the large areas of uncultivated land in Great Britain are not given up to the breeding of goats on a large scale, since these hardy animals will thrive on rough, hilly lands. Apart from the value of the meat, it might be a paying proposition to rear large herds of goats for the supply of milk (which is more nourishing than cows') and skins. Leather-dressers are, therefore, dependent on imported supplies, of which the principal sources are India (North-Western District), Mexico, Arabia, Africa, South America, and several European countries.

Goat skins from the main sources of supply vary very much in quality-even those produced in the same country. In India, for example, skins may be obtained in some districts which can be made into leather to sell at about 5d. per square foot; from another district, when finished into the same kind of leather, say glazed kid, they may be worth 1s. 4d.[1] per foot. Fineness and clearness of grain and good substance are the main essentials of a first-class goat-skin leather; unfortunately these qualities are rarely combined in one class of skin, and there is a decided surplus of light thin skins which are hardly saleable, even for ladies' shoes. Some American shoemakers overcome this difficulty by pasting a piece of cloth on the back of the skin. In fairness to the buyer, the boots made of such leather should be specially marked, as the wearing quality of a backed thin leather is not to be compared with one naturally stout.

[1] It must be understood that, owing to the war, these prices have been greatly increased.

The skins of goats are used for many purposes besides the manufacture of the famous glacé kid leather; gloves, moroccos for bookbinding, upholstery for furniture, fancy articles such as purses, pocket-books, bags, and ladies' belts all require large quantities of goat and kid skins. It may be pointed out here, however, that quite nine-tenths of the so-called kid gloves are made of lamb and sheep skins. In appearance, there is very little difference between the real kid and the lamb skin gloves, but the former are more durable and warmer in wear than the latter.

With an enormous range of qualities, it is a difficult task for the goat-skin dresser to find the most suitable sorts for his trade. The skins used in the glove industry are largely obtained from the Near Eastern countries, Arabia, Austria, Spain, and the Cape. The selections best suited to the making of glazed and "patent" (japanned) kid are found in the North-Western provinces of India, Brazil, China, Russia (especially the Asiatic provinces), Mexico, the Cape, and Arabia. The Indian goats known as the Patnas, which are collected in the district of Behar, are commonly supposed to be the best in the world, chiefly because of their fine grain and stout substance; but the best Brazilian and Mexican skins are equally good in quality. The best moroccos for fancy articles are made from Continental skins, and in this respect Germany has the great advantage of a good supply of native skins. Norway and Spain also provide skins suitable for real morocco leather. A very large quantity of Indian-tanned goat skins are imported into European countries and dressed for "morocco" leather. There should be a distinctive name for this class of leather, as, although it is similar in appearance, it is not nearly so good in quality as the real morocco.

In addition to cattle hides, sheep, and goat skins, which are the main supply of raw material for leather, other kinds of hides and skins are utilised. Horse hides, which, in the United Kingdom, are graded according to size and quality in four or five selections and sold by the piece, are largely used on the Continent, and especially in Germany; nearly all of the British production being sold to that country. When chrome tanned, these hides produce quite a serviceable upper leather of good wearing quality, but, owing to their somewhat loose texture, the characteristic grain of box calf cannot be reproduced naturally, and the surface of the leather has, therefore, to be printed. This style of finished leather does not meet with the favour of British boot manufacturers, and the industry has not been greatly developed in consequence. In view of the increasing cost of other kinds of leather, however, more attention may be paid to that made from horse hide, but the supply of this raw material is very small compared to the production on the Continent, where horse flesh is consumed freely. Russia produces large quantities of horse hides and colt skins, most of which are exported to the United States of America, where they are made chiefly into japanned, or so-called "patent," leather, which commands a very high price in relation to the cost of the raw material.

Next in importance to horse hides is the pig skin, which produces a wonderfully tough leather. The pig skin leather industry is chiefly confined to Scotland and Germany, the reason being that the skins are left on the carcases in the other parts of the world. On the average, a pig skin is worth about 6s., yet it is seldom removed from the carcase. One reason is the great difficulty of flaying the animal; it appears to be almost impossible by present methods to remove the skin without cutting away a large quantity of fat, and the value of the skin compared to the loss of weight of the meat offers very little inducement to remove the skin, in addition to which, the custom of leaving the rind on bacon and pork effectually prevents any attempt at present to increase the supply of pig skins. This is a great loss to the leather trade, for the pig skin is particularly suitable for saddles and various kinds of strong leather goods. Imitation pig-skin leather is made from hides, shoulders, bellies, or persians, but real pig skin is distinguished from the imitation by its peculiarly marked grain, formed of groups of three small holes which penetrate well into the skin and form part of the sheaths of the pig's bristles.

Among other skins useful for leather are those of the wallaby, kangaroo, dog, lizard, crocodile, alligator, ichneumon, frog (Japanese), deer, antelope, and chamois, while it is said that even rabbit skins have been pressed into service in Germany, though they cannot have much value owing to their small size and thin substance. Dog-skin leather wears well, mainly on account of the large amount of natural grease present in the skin, but the supplies are naturally small. The hides of the walrus, elephant, rhinoceros, hippopotamus, and other wild animals are also tanned in small quantities, walrus leather being well adapted for knife and sword polishing.

The mammals also contribute their quota to the supply of raw material of the leather trade, the seal perhaps, being the most important. This refers to the hairy seal hunted off the North American coast.

The raw skins are shipped chiefly from Newfoundland, where the industry of seal fishing is well organised and provides employment for about 6,000 men. The seal caught in the North Atlantic Ocean is hairy and quite distinct from the fur seal captured in the Arctic Ocean off Alaska. The skin of the hair seal is only suitable for making into leather, but there is a layer of fat underneath it which furnishes a valuable raw material for the manufacture of oils and soap. The skins are salted and shipped to America and England. They are easily distinguished from other kinds of commercial hides and skins by the oily appearance of the flesh side.

According to an American Consular Report, the results of the fishing during the season 1913 were satisfactory. The total number of seals captured was 272,965, which were valued at £98,800. The number of skins exported was 212,285, valued at £64,300, of which the United States of America bought 151,355, the United Kingdom 60,754, and Canada 176.

The porpoise, or sea hog, has a very useful hide which, when dressed, makes a tough leather suitable for laces. The hides of other cetaceous mammals, such as the whale and narwhal, are convertible into useful leather. The British "porpoise" laces are generally made from the skin of the white whale (*beluga*).

Defects of Raw Hides and Skins

A remarkable feature of the leather trade is the great waste due to the careless preparation of a large number of hides and skins. Naturally, owing to their greatly increased value in recent years, there has been a decided improvement, but much loss occurs every day from damage to hides which ought to be avoided. The chief faults are in flaying and curing, but there are other important defects due to natural causes.

Bad flaying may be due (1) to cutting holes in the hides or skins; (2) to "scoring" or "siding" (*i.e.*, cutting into the hide without going completely through), this generally occurring in the flanks or sides which are the most difficult parts of the hide to remove from the carcase; and (3) to mis-shaping the hide, which ought to be left square.

Any or all of these defects may be found in a single hide. Despite the active work of several proprietors of hide markets and the tanners' federations the proportion of badly-flayed hides in England constitutes a serious loss, which, however, may not fall directly on either the butcher or the tanner, for the former may save in wages by employing an inexperienced slaughterman, while the tanner pays a reduced price for the hide.

The losses due to bad flaying and curing in the United Kingdom are mainly attributable to the butchers' preference to kill these beasts in their own back-yard rather than in a public abattoir. Many of these small private slaughterhouses ought to be condemned by the authorities; but very few people outside those immediately interested have taken the trouble to inspect a modern public abattoir where everything is provided to carry on the work expeditiously and hygienically. On the Continent, where the conservatism of traders is not permitted to interfere with the public welfare to such an extent as it is in England, public abattoirs have become quite a feature in many cities, and one of the principal results of the system has been a remarkable improvement in the preparation of raw hides and skins for the tanner. In fact, a mechanical method of flaying has been invented in Paris, and is used extensively at the public abattoirs, by which hides are removed from cattle without a single mark or scratch. The method is known as *dépouille mécanique* (mechanical flaying) and consists in forcibly removing, by means of a windlass worked by electric power, the portions of hide which adhere firmly to the carcase and which are found over the ribs, the buttocks, and the tail. The remaining part of the hide can be easily removed with the ordinary butchers' flaying knife or with a heavy hammer of special design. The apparatus required to carry out the mechanical method of flaying, beyond the fixtures in the abattoirs where the process is adopted, consist of two lengths of chain to hold the carcase firmly, two special hammers, and one pair of strong pincers; the cost of one set is about £4. Mr. Gaston Tainturier, of Paris, is the inventor of this system, which has added thousands of pounds to the incomes of Parisian butchers.

Figure 1 is from a photograph taken at the Islington (London) Abattoir, where a demonstration of the process was given by Mr. Tainturier in February, 1913.

Naturally, this method cannot be adopted in small slaughterhouses in back-yards, but is readily adaptable to public abattoirs, where practically all of the heavy work is done by electrical power. This exemplifies only one of several advantages of modern abattoirs over private slaughterhouses.

Although it cannot be expected that the English butchers will readily change their prejudice against modern abattoirs, they are slowly but gradually improving the flaying process in view of the high prices paid for perfect hides. The most progressive of the proprietors of the English hide markets are offering money prizes to slaughtermen for the best flayed hides. Strictly speaking, this encouragement should come from the butcher, who receives the benefit of increased prices for hides removed without a scratch. The Tainturier system, however, gives better results, no matter how well the hides are removed with the knife. The method is not patented, and it is open to anyone to adopt it merely for the cost of the apparatus, yet, despite this gain, no butcher outside France and Belgium has yet adopted the method, although the trade is losing hundreds of pounds every week through bad flaying.

Several other systems of improved flaying have been devised, and some of them patented, but very few have been adopted on a practical scale. One of the most useful consists of fixing a safeguard about a quarter of an inch from the edge of the knife; this prevents the possibility of cutting holes into the hide, although it does not, of course, prevent scoring, which is a serious defect in hides made into sole leather. A safe method is to use a sharp knife of hard wood, such as hickory, which has been successfully tried in one of the large American meat-packing establishments. The hides from these abattoirs are generally well-flayed, properly cured, and closely trimmed, with the result that they command higher prices than any other class of salted

hides. The quotations for "packer" hides are followed with keen interest by tanners in all parts
of the world.

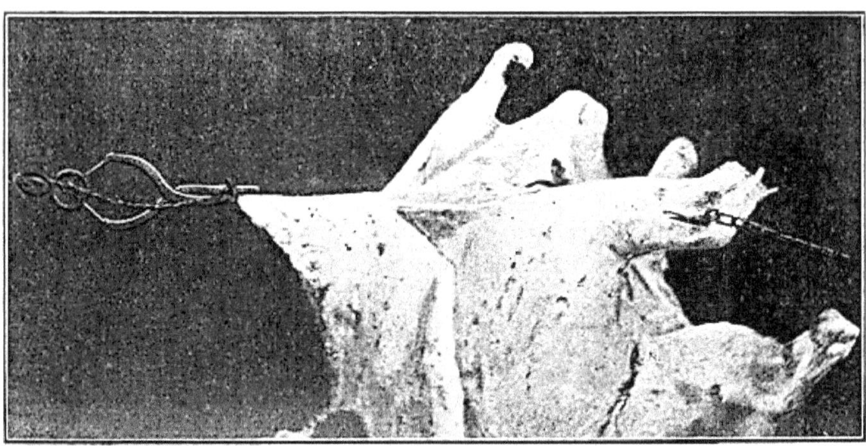

Fig. 1
MECHANICAL FLAYING
(*dépouille mécanique*)]

Another useful method of preventing damage to the hides by cuts with a knife is that invented
by Mr. E. Pim, a Liverpool hide factor. The apparatus used is known as the tail extractor. It
is of simple construction, consisting of four pieces of iron riveted together loosely in the shape
of a diamond with a clamp attached to secure the tail. The hide is then forcibly removed from
the tail and the buttocks by pulling it downward (Fig. 2). The importance of this operation
can be gauged from the fact that by the use of the butcher's knife both of these parts of the
hide are often cut very badly.

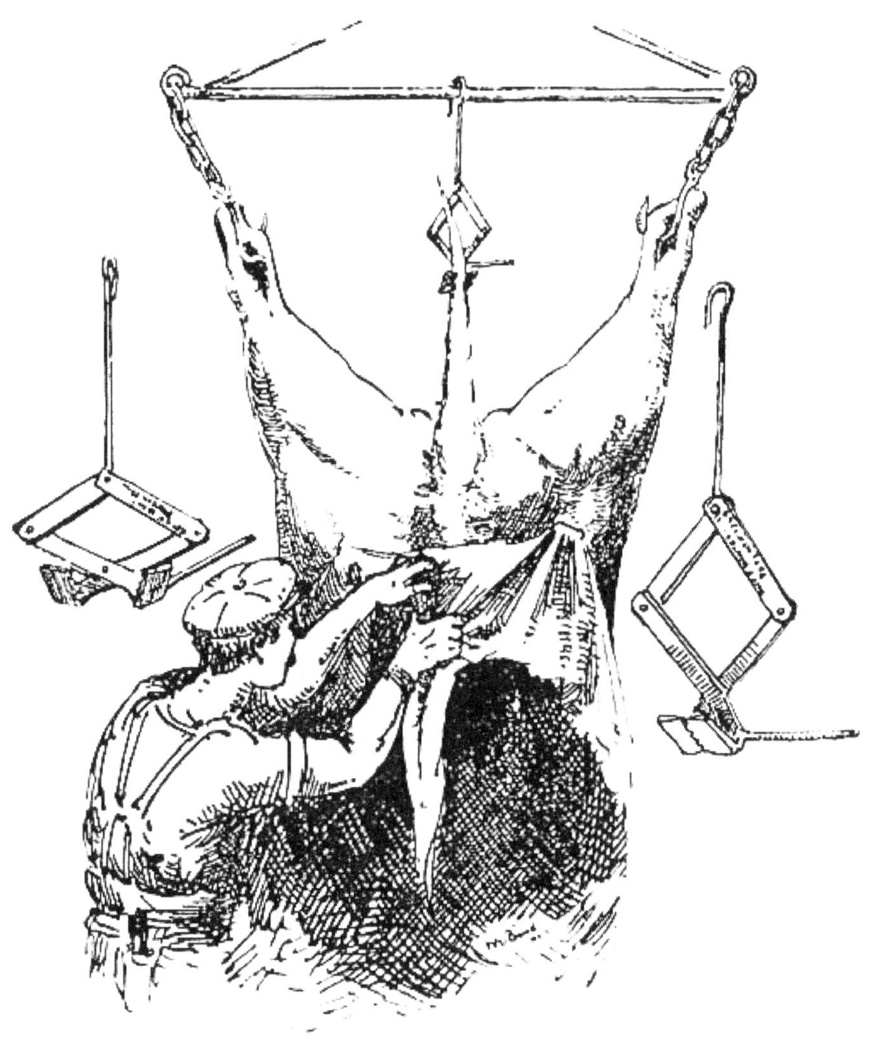

Fig. 2

PIM'S SYSTEM OF FLAYING

Even the apparently trivial matter of removing the hide from the cheeks and face is economically important, for, unless those parts are removed so as to get the maximum surface, they are only fit to be cut off and thrown in a pit with other pieces and roundings which are made into glue.

Imperfect preservation is another serious form of damage to hides and one that cannot be easily remedied in some of the hot climates. Hides and skins may be simply dried, salted and dried, wet-salted, treated with arsenic solution and dried, brined or pickled with acid and salt; of these methods the last-named is the most effective, but is not practicable, or, at least, has not yet been applied practically to the cure of hides and calf skins. Salt is not available, or is too costly in most tropical countries; hence, Chinese, Indian, Mexican, Colombian, and Arabian hides and skins are generally exported in a dry condition. Even when the hides are dried under the best conditions in a cool and shady place, they are of less value than a fresh or a wet-salted hide, owing to a certain loss of gelatinous matter in softening them before they can be placed in the lime liquors. But it not infrequently happens that hides are dried by exposure to the hot sun, or perhaps in a strong current of air. In either case, the hide is much reduced in value and may be irreparably ruined. The effect of submitting hides to these conditions is that the exterior surface becomes rapidly dry and, naturally, contracted, so that the air or heat cannot reach the interior, which retains moisture. This moist inner layer may be quite thin, but it contains sufficient nutrient to develop putrefactive organisms, so that when the hide is soaked in water it practically falls to pieces. The effect of hot sun or heat of any kind is, of course, disastrous to raw hides and skins, and there have been not a few claims on shipping companies as the result of storing hides near the boilers of ships.

Salt is almost invariably used for curing both hides and calf skins, but though it is a good preservative it has one or two minor defects. It contains too much water, and is liable to contain traces of iron which is inimical to both raw hides and leather in process of manufacture. Common salt is also liable to cause stains which cannot be removed in later processes, and which are even accentuated in the tan liquors. One trade chemist attributes these stains to the presence of calcium sulphate (Ca. SO_4) or gypsum in the salt, which is converted into calcium phosphate by the action of the phosphoric acid in the nuclei of the hide on the sulphate of calcium. Another well-known technical chemist is certain that stains are produced by the growth of bacteria, and to prove his assertion prepared in gelatine several cultures from salt-stained skins. Practical men generally attribute the stains to the presence of blood on the hides or skins at the time of curing, and the majority of the stains are probably due to this cause, although the presence of calcium sulphate as an impurity of the salt would undoubtedly contribute to this defect. Blood contains a percentage of iron, and, with other extraneous matters, should be washed from the hides before salting them.

Fortunately, chemists have lately paid attention to the advantages of the use of pure salt in various industries, with the result that at least two chemically pure products are now available. The use of these salts should be general for the cure of hides and skins, as they are quite dry, and, therefore, easily spread. As a curing agent, they are much more effective and lasting than common salt.

The use of glauber salts (Na_2 SO_4) is recommended by the International Commission for the Preservation, Cure, and Disinfection of Hides and Skins instead of ordinary salt, where the latter is unobtainable. The preparation of a sterilised salt, however, renders its export a practical proposition to almost any part of the world.

Although the loss due to bad curing and flaying is very great, it is quite small compared with the damage caused by natural defects.

The ravages of disease cause a great wastage of hides and skins, as animals infected with anthrax are immediately destroyed and cremated in all civilised countries, while, in Great Britain, foot-and-mouth disease is kept in check by the same drastic method. In many other countries, the infected cattle are isolated, treated with an antiseptic hoof-and-mouth wash and generally cured, as it is a mild fever which soon runs its course, although it is very contagious. The germ of foot-and-mouth disease has not yet been discovered, for the most powerful microscope fails to reveal its presence, but cattle readily show the complaint, as their hoofs and mouths become covered with swollen lesions.

Another kind of fever, known as "tick," was prevalent in the southern part of the United States, but this disease was eventually eliminated by systematically "dipping" the cattle three or four times a year. The cattle "dip" used effectually prevented the ravages of the fly which caused the disease. A similar method has of late years been adopted in South Africa, with the result that cattle-raising in that country is developing rapidly.

Anthrax is due to the presence of *bacillus anthracis*, a vegetable organism of Siberian origin. Dry Chinese and Russian hides are specially liable to contain the spores of anthrax, and, as the disease proves fatal to workmen infected by it unless treatment with anti-anthrax serum be given in the early stages, hides and skins from infected areas should be disinfected before shipment. The method proposed by Mr. A. Seymour-Jones, which consists in treating hides with very dilute formic acid and one part of bichloride of mercury in 1,000 of water, and afterwards with a saturated solution of salt solution (.02 per cent.) of bichloride of mercury, seems to be the most effective without damaging the hides.

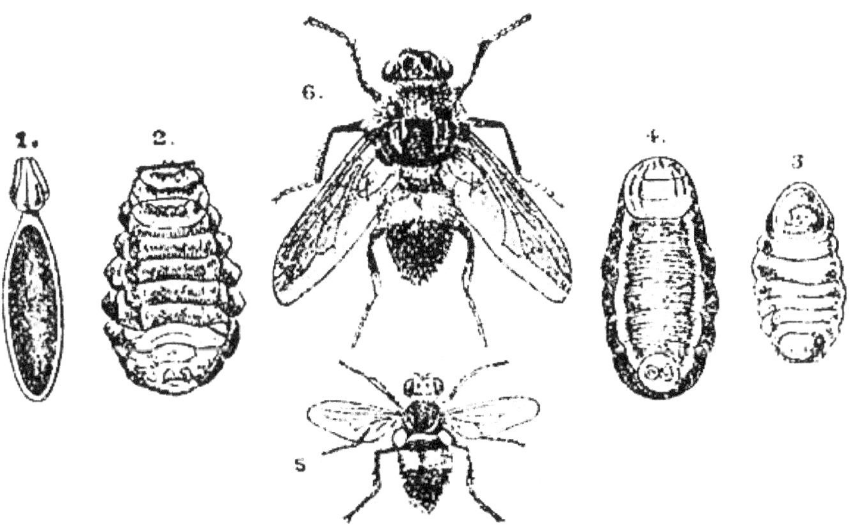

WARBLE FLY
(1) Egg, (2) Larva, (3 and 4) Chrysalides,
(5) Natural form of fly, (6) Magnified fly.

A peculiar natural defect is found in many South American goat skins, especially the Brazilian, which are often badly scratched by the animals rubbing themselves against cactus plants. Although, perhaps, more of an artificial than a natural defect, the scratches caused by cattle rubbing their hides against barbed wire constitute a serious, but easily avoidable, loss. Such a barbarous system of fencing ought never to be used.

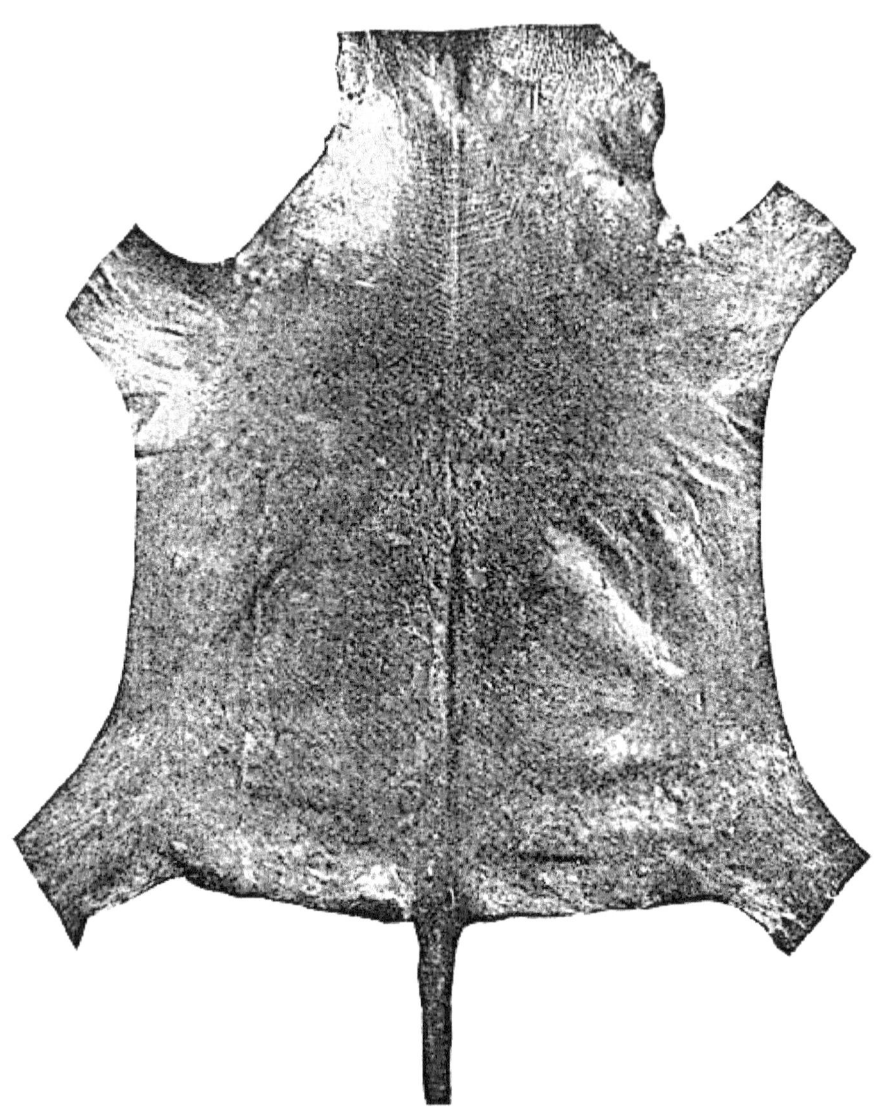

A KIP CONTAINING 584 HOLES CAUSED BY THE WARBLE FLY
(The skin belongs to W. D. Mark & Sons, Hide Factors, Newcastle.)

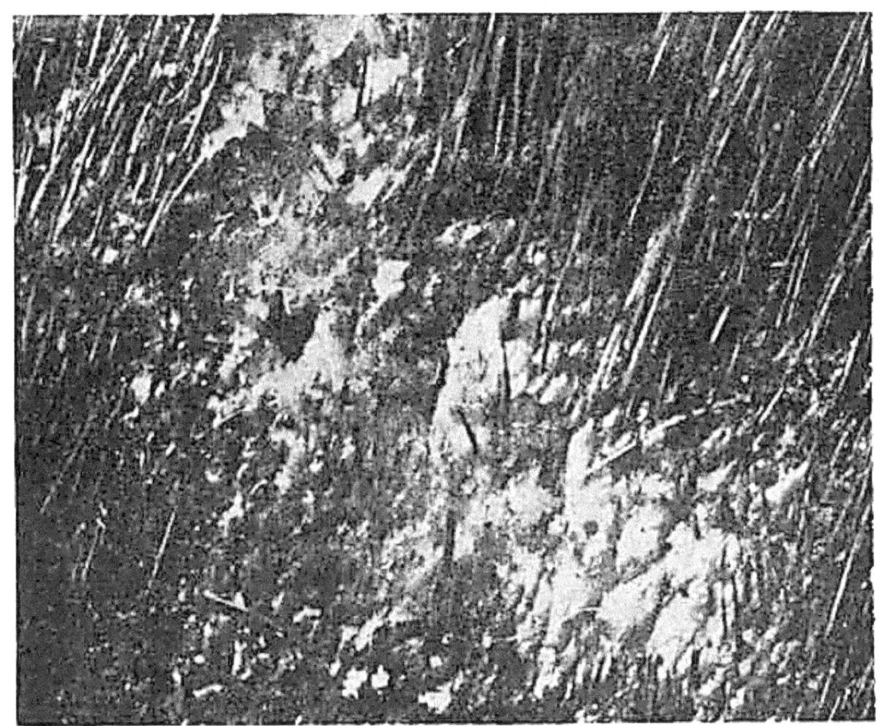

HOLE IN COW HIDE, MADE BY THE GRUB OF THE WARBLE FLY
(Magnified fifteen times)

The most serious loss in connection with hides and skins, however, is caused by the warble flies, *hypoderma bovis* and *hypoderma lineatum*, which lay their eggs on the hides of cattle. It has been a debatable point for some years as to whether these eggs hatched and burrowed their way into the hides from the exterior or were licked and swallowed by the cattle and, after traversing the digestive tract, pierced the hide from the interior. Professor Carpenter, who has been experimenting a number of years for the Department of Agriculture for Ireland, has succeeded in taking a remarkable photograph (Fig. 3) which proves that the larvae penetrate the hide from the exterior. These develop within the hide and often penetrate to the flesh before they fall out to the ground and change into the fly.

The most effective way of getting rid of the pest is to destroy the larvae, either by cutting them out and crushing them under foot, or by piercing them with a hot needle. No satisfactory dressing has yet been found, but Prof. Carpenter states that sulphur dioxide is effectual, if a good method of applying it can be devised.

While sheep skins are immune from the attacks of the warble fly, they are often damaged by the blow-fly, lice, keds, and ticks; by scab caused by the action of a mite or acarus; and by "cockle," which causes a wrinkled grain. The origin of cockle is not definitely known, but it is a seasonal defect which begins to show on a large number of skins in December and does not disappear until the sheep are shorn in the following spring.

CHAPTER III TANNING MATERIALS

Tanning materials are derived from the vegetable, mineral, and animal kingdoms.

The vegetable materials used are woods, barks, shrubs, leaves, and fruits, either in their natural state or in the form of extracts. The majority of the minerals have a more or less tanning effect on animal fibres, but the principal are basic chrome salts, formaldehyde, alum and salt. Titanium, iron, cerium and potassium salts also convert skins into leather, but are not yet used commercially.

The animal matters that will convert skins into leather consist of oxidised oils (chamois leather), fats, and brains (crown, Helvetia, or Preller's leather).

Each of these classes of tanning materials has characteristic effects which render them easily distinguishable. The use of combinations of vegetable and mineral tannins has lately increased, and it is possible that the blending of the two classes of materials may produce an ideal tannage for certain classes of leather. In fact, this result is already claimed for a chemically combined tanning material which, according to the American patent, is prepared by the following method: 125 lb. of solid quebracho extract is dissolved in the same weight of hot water and allowed to cool; 16 lb. of commercial caustic soda dissolved in two or three times its weight of water is added, and the mixture agitated about half an hour; 150 lb. of chromium sulphate is then added. In this way an insoluble tannate of chrome is produced, but, on boiling and agitating, it changes to a greenish brown colour and forms a sulphotannate of chrome. The combination of the alum tannage and gambier (a vegetable extract) has been used successfully for years past. Another combination which has given good practical results is the tannage with alum and chrome salts in the manufacture of glove leather.

The vegetable materials containing tannin should be arranged botanically, but the following classification is simpler for practical purposes.

Natural Tanning Materials

1. *Barks.* —Oak, Hemlock, Pine, Fir, Alder, Khaki, Willow, Cork, Mimosa or Wattle, Babool, Larch, Mangrove, Spruce, Elm, Birch, Pomegranate, Cebil.

2. *Leaves, Twigs, etc.* —Sumach, Mangrove, Mango, Eucalyptus, Pistacia, Lentiscus.

3. *Roots.* —Canaigre, Palmetto.

4. *Fruits.* —Myrobalans, Valonia, Divi-Divi, Cascalote, Mangosteen, Pomegranate, Celavinia, Bablah, Algarobilla.

5. *Excrescences.* —Gall Nuts, Chinese Galls, Pistacia Galls, Tamarisk Galls.

Tanning Extracts

1. *Woods.* —Oak, Quebracho, Hemlock, Chestnut, Mimosa, Mangrove, Spruce.
2. *Barks.* —Oak, Wattle or Mimosa, Larch.
3. *Shrubs, Leaves, etc.* —Gambier, Cutch, Catechu, Kino, Sumach.
4. *Fruits.* —Myrobalans, Valonia.
5. *Roots.* —Palmetto.

Of these materials, only about twenty are of much importance commercially, the principal being oak, chestnut, quebracho, hemlock, valonia, gambier, myrobalans, mimosa or wattle, sumach, mangrove, divi-divi, spruce, larch, and babool.

OAK BARK (*quercus robur*) is still an important material, but is rarely used alone. The bark from English oaks contains from 8-14 per cent. of tannin (quercitannic acid) as estimated by the impregnation of a standardised hide powder in a given quantity of the tanning material in solution. Owing to its weakness in tannin compared with other materials, oak bark tans very slowly. Used for sole leather, it would not produce the essential quality of firmness and solidity, and it is now customary to use a stronger tanning material, such as valonia, or valonia extract, or gambier in the latter stages of the process. This is the nearest approach to the pure oak bark tannage of former days, and, if carefully regulated, is a great improvement on the old method.

If dressing hides and calf skins required for boot upper leather are bark-tanned, the tannage is often completed in a sumach liquor, the object in this case being to lighten the colour so that the leather can be dyed evenly.

In England, oak bark is harvested in April and May, when the sap rises in the tree. Rings are cut round the tree soon after it is felled and the bark is peeled from the tree with a special tool which is forced between the bark and the wood. It is peeled in narrow strips about 3 ft. in length, and on delivery to the tannery is stacked in huge ricks. If harvested in a good, dry condition, the bark is said to improve with age, although analytical tests have shown that there is always a certain loss of tannin. An old rick is much darker in colour than a new one, owing to exposure to the air. Coppice bark from young trees is preferred by tanners, as it is free from ross and generally contains more tannin than the rough bark.

In view of the modern demand for materials in extract form, English oak bark would almost certainly be preferred in the form of a concentrated liquid, if the supply of the raw material was plentiful within a limited area. During the last few years it has not met with a ready sale, owing to the large supply of other materials, but it would doubtless regain some of its former popularity if it were prepared in the form of an extract containing about 25 per cent. of tannin. The only oak bark extract on the market is the American chestnut oak (*quercus prinus*).

OAK WOOD is very largely used for the manufacture of tanning extract, especially in Hungary and Canada. The extract contains from 24-28 per cent. of tannin, and is extensively used in the tannage of heavy leathers, as it strengthens the liquors and hastens the process, while keeping the quality of the leather at a high standard.

VALONIA (*quercus aegilops*) is the acorn cups of an oak tree which grows abundantly in Asia Minor and the Greek Archipelago. No other part but the acorn cups is exported. The harvest in Asia Minor takes place in August, when the fruit ripens and the cups can be easily beaten from the trees. They are left to dry on the ground and are then sent to stores in seaport towns, and principally to Smyrna. The drying is still further completed in spacious warehouses, where the cups are spread out and turned over until fermentation ceases. During this process the acorns shrink and are rejected. The cups should be perfectly dried and very hard before export. The Turkish valonia contains from 30 to 35 per cent. of tannin, and is of much better quality than the Greek, which is usually harvested before it is ripe, and, therefore, contains the acorn. As the acorn has practically no tannin value, the Greek valonia contains only 25 to 28 per cent. tannin. There are several grades of valonia, the best going to Russia, Austria, and Italy. English tanners seem to prefer the lower qualities at present, probably because the price is much less than that of the best grade.

The beard of the valonia cup is much richer in tannin than the shell, and, as several of the spines become detached during the storage of the material, there is always a certain quantity of beard (*trillo*) on offer. This may contain up to 42 per cent. of tannin, but its price is usually the same as that of ordinary valonia. Of late years, very large quantities of valonia have been made into extract at two works in Smyrna. The production of extract will no doubt increase, with a corresponding reduction in the export of the raw material. The great advantages of the extract over the natural cup are its superior strength of tannin (60 to 65 per cent.), easier solubility, uniformity of quality, lower cost per unit of tan, and guaranteed purity.

Valonia is well adapted for the tannage of sole leather in conjunction with oak bark, for it deposits a heavy bloom (ellagic acid), imparts weight and solidity, and increases the resistance of the leather to moisture.

THE CHESTNUT TREE (*castanea vesca*) probably provides the next tanning material of importance. This must not be confused with the chestnut oak, an American tree which also yields a very useful tannin. The chestnut is indigenous to the South of France and Italy, where the forests have been considerably reduced in size to meet the great demand for this popular tanning material. The greater part of the denuded forests have not been replanted with the chestnut, as the land has been put under cultivation whenever possible. A further depletion has been caused by the ravages of an insect, which turns the interior of the wood quite black and renders it unfit for tanning purposes. It will, naturally, be several years before the supply is exhausted, even if no reafforestation is undertaken. As it is the most important tanning material grown in France, and the chestnuts are used as a food, steps may be taken to cultivate the trees on areas unsuitable for agriculture. Liquid chestnut extract contains from 30 to 32 per cent. of tannin, and, when decolorised, gives a light brown colour to the leather. It is rarely, if ever, used alone, but generally in conjunction with quebracho, valonia or myrobalan extracts.

THE CHESTNUT OAK TREE is indigenous to America and the wood yields a very good tanning extract, containing up to 30 per cent. of tannin. This material is the principal tanning agent used in America, where the tannages are roughly classified in three sections: (1) oak, (2) hemlock, and (3) the union (*i.e.*, a mixture of hemlock and oak). American tanners also use other materials to a smaller extent, chiefly for blending with the principal tannins. Quebracho and spruce extracts are specially favoured.

QUEBRACHO COLORADO is a tree indigenous to South America, the best wood for tanning purposes being found in the Gran Chaco district in the north of Argentina, and in Uruguay. The wood contains from 17 to 22 per cent. of tannin, and is so hard and heavy that it sinks in water. In fact, its name is derived from two Portuguese words meaning "axe-breaker."

After felling the trees, they are cut up into logs about 4 ft. in length and either exported in this state to Hamburg, Havre, and Liverpool, or sent to the numerous factories in close proximity to the forests to be made into extract, in which an enormous trade has of late years been developed. Very little of the natural material is now used, as, even after cutting the wood into chips, the tannin is extracted only with great difficulty, whereas the extract can be treated with sulphites, alkalies, or neradol (the artificial tannin) to render it easily soluble, besides which the concentration of the material raises the percentage of its tannin to 65 or even 70 per cent. Owing, perhaps, to faulty preparation, this tanning extract was not well received at first, but it is now among the principal tannins and increases in importance every year.

MYROBALANS is the unripe fruit of an Indian tree (*terminalia chebula*) and contains from 35 to 40 per cent. of tannin which gives a light colour to leather. This material is useful both for light and heavy leathers, but is generally used in admixture with other tannins. It deposits much bloom (ellagic acid) and is largely used for brightening the dark colour produced by other tannins. A large quantity of this material is now made into extracts, which are more convenient to handle and more uniform in strength of tannin. Natural myrobalans have the appearance of shrivelled nutmegs, except that they are yellowish in colour; they are very hard and require a special milling machine to reduce them to powder. The quality of myrobalan nuts varies in different districts, the best being Bhimlies and Jubbalpores.

Sumach is a valuable tanning material, and is used for a large proportion of the light and fancy leathers. It is a small bush plant which grows in Italy, Spain, Southern France, America, and Algeria, but of the numerous varieties the Sicilian (*rhus coriaria*) is by far the most important. Sumach is one of the few materials cultivated on an extensive scale; most tanning materials are derived from natural sources and, chiefly owing to the length of time before trees reach maturity, it would not be a paying proposition to cultivate them. The sumach shrubs are propagated from small cuttings and the leaves can be picked at the end of the first year, but it is better to allow the shrubs to become more firmly established before stripping them. The leaves are dried and sometimes exported whole, especially for the use of the silk manufacturers in Lyons; but they are more often ground to a fine powder. All sumachs should be ventilated to remove foreign matters and all traces of iron, which would cause dark bluish stains on the leather. "Ventilation" is effected by passing currents of air, preferably with a fan, through a narrow room, when the pure sumach is sent forward, while the heavier particles of dirt and small pieces of wood remain behind. Sometimes the process is repeated, and the best brands of sumach are generally described as "pure, extra ventilated." As far as possible, the male plants (*mascolino sommacco*) are cultivated in Sicily, where the best sumach is grown. Female sumach (*femminello sommacco*), grown in parts of Italy, is weaker in tannin than the male, but is rarely sold separately. The serious amount of adulteration formerly practised by the admixture of inferior plants, and particularly of lentisco (*pistacia lentisco*) led to the Italian Government taking strong action a few years ago, and it is now possible, for a very small sum, to have any consignment inspected and analysed by the Government. Lentisco is now sold separately and is used for common work.

Sumach has been successfully introduced into Australia, but its development is retarded owing to difficulties of labour, which render competition with the European product almost impossible. An inferior sumach (*rhus glabra*) is grown in America, chiefly in the State of Virginia. It contains from 15 to 20 per cent. of tannin, and produces a darker coloured leather than Sicilian, the best qualities of which contain 27 to 30 per cent. of tannin.

A useful test for finding out if a sumach has been adulterated is to treat a small quantity with strong nitric acid, which destroys the structure of the leaves. The mass is washed and neutralised with an alkali, when the appearance of the midrib and veins of the leaves of the common adulterants are easily recognised.

Sumach is not so much used for shoe upper leather as it formerly was, but it is the best tanning agent for many kinds of fancy light leathers, such as bookbinding, calf, and skivers (the grain of split sheep skins), moroccos, furniture leather, etc. It is also less subject to the action of the air and gaslight than any other tanning material, and is strongly recommended for tanning purposes by a special committee appointed by the Society of Arts to enquire into causes of the rapid decay of leather bindings. Sumach is very useful for brightening up the colour of leather tanned with darker tannins, and is frequently used for improving the colour of both dressing and sole leather. By itself, it yields an almost white leather which affords a good foundation for the most delicate shades.

Gambier or Terra Japonica (*uncaria gambir*) is a crude extract of a shrub indigenous to the Malay Peninsula. Nearly the whole of the production is shipped from Singapore. The leaves and twigs are boiled in an iron vessel, and when the mass has become syrupy it is strained through a rough sieve into a shallow tub, where it is cooled. The liquor is stirred while cooling and rapidly thickens. Before it sets, it is cut into 1 in. cubes and thoroughly dried. Good qualities contain from 50-65 per cent. of tannin. An inferior product, called "block gambier," is made by allowing the syrupy mass to set in large blocks weighing about 2 cwt. each. These are packed in coarse matting. The strength of tannin varies from 30 to 40 per cent. Gambier is a good tanning material, but its use has been declining for some years past owing to its being frequently adulterated with sago and other farinaceous plants. However, a pure gambier extract, manufactured on the latest scientific principles, has been placed on the market, and there will undoubtedly be a revival of the use of this valuable tannin. This pure gambier is prepared at Asahan, in Sumatra, and is guaranteed to contain a minimum of 38 per cent. of tannin.

Gambier can be used to advantage in keeping up the strength of bark liquors in the tannage of sole leather and hastening the process, while it may be used alone for the tannage of boot upper leather and dressing hides. It produces an exceptionally mellow and plump leather. It is preferable, however, to complete a gambier tannage with a little oak wood or quebracho extract, in order to fix the tannin principle of gambier, which, perhaps on account of its viscosity, does not readily combine with the fibres of the skin.

Mangrove or Mangle, a tree found on the coasts of several tropical countries, yields a useful bark for tanning purposes. At low tide, these trees show their great arched roots standing high above the ground. The best varieties, the *ceriops* species, are found in the East Indies and Bengal, and the bark of these is said to contain sometimes nearly 40 per cent. of tannin. Other varieties contain from 15 to 25 per cent. The bark is generally made into a solid extract, or "cutch," in which form it contains more than 60 per cent. of tannin, It is useful to blend with other materials, such as oak wood, chestnut, and quebracho extracts, but used by itself it imparts a strong reddish colour to the leather. Some of the Indian varieties are used as dyeing materials, and act as a satisfactory mordant in dyeing leather a dark shade.

Mimosa or Wattle trees, which belong to the *acacia* species, yield bark rich in tannin. Australia is the native country of several varieties, including the Black Wattle (*acacia pycnantha*), the Golden Wattle (*A. longifolia*), and the Green Wattle (*A. decurrens*).

The bark contains from 20 to 45 per cent. of tannin. The cultivation of wattle in Australia seems to have declined, owing to the high cost of labour and inability to compete with the mimosa bark imported from South Africa, where it is cultivated on a very large scale and where labour conditions are more favourable for the growers, as is clearly shown by the fact that the wattle growers in Australia successfully petitioned the Government a short time ago to place a duty of £1 10s. per ton on the imported bark.

The introduction of the industry into South Africa was quite an interesting adventure. A Mr. Vanderplank brought the seeds from Australia to England about seventy years ago, and afterwards took them to South Africa, where, in recognition of certain services a few months after his arrival, he was granted a farm by the Dutch Government. He then planted the seeds of the black wattle, which grew so well that it was only a question of developing the industry. It was some years before any African bark was exported, and only £11 worth was shipped in 1886. In 1911, the exports had risen to £288,000.

Wattle trees can be grown on soil that is unsuitable for agriculture, and there is every prospect of the industry expanding in South Africa, where a factory has lately been established for the purpose of converting the bark into an extract, which, it is said, will contain between 50 and 60 per cent. of tannin. By far the greater proportion of wattle bark is still exported in the natural form, ground or chopped, and packed into bags weighing about 1 cwt. each. Before the European War nearly the whole of the bark was shipped to Hamburg, English tanners taking very little interest in it, although it was largely used by German tanners. But since the supplies of the materials favoured by British tanners have become somewhat restricted, attention has been drawn to the value of mimosa bark.

Divi-Divi (*caesalpinia coriaria*) is the dried pods of a Central American tree. It has also been successfully cultivated in India. The pods are rich in tannin, containing anything from 40 50 per cent., but its value is discounted by its liability to fermentation, which, however, may be checked to some extent by the use of antiseptics, such as carbolic acid, formaldehyde, or by the addition of synthetic tannin, neradol. If this tendency to fermentation and oxidation of the colouring matter could be checked completely, divi-divi would be a valuable material, as it makes a firm leather of good colour. When dried, the pods curl up in the shape of the letters S and C. The tannin is found in the husks of the pod. The seeds, which contain no tannin, are so hard that it has not yet been found profitable to extract the oil from them. Very similar tanning materials to divi-divi are cascalote, indigenous to Mexico, and algarobilla (*caesalpinia brevifolia*) which grows in Chili. Cascalote is chiefly used by Mexican tanners and is rarely exported. Algarobilla is not available in large quantities, otherwise it would be largely used in Great Britain, as it does not ferment so readily as divi-divi, and is even richer in tannin.

CELAVINIA (also spelt celavina and cevalina) has been on the English market since 1905, but has only lately been sold in large quantities. The scarcity of some of the popular tanning materials since the outbreak of the European War resulted in enquiries for materials that were very little known, and celavinia has proved worthy of attention. It consists of the seed pods of the tree *caesalpinia tinctoria*, which grows abundantly in certain districts of Central and South America. The pod is from 4 to 6 in. long and is flaky when dried. It contains 30 to 32 per cent, of tannin of the pyrogallol class, and gives a very light-coloured and almost white leather. It is the only pyrogallol tannin which does not deposit bloom, or ellagic acid, on the leather. It may be used as a substitute for sumach in tanning, but has not the same bleaching effect in the retanning process. A tanning extract of celavinia would be useful for some classes of light leathers, where paleness of tint is important. It is difficult to make a second extraction of tannin in the case of the natural material, as, after the first extraction, it forms a soft pulp, through which water will not easily percolate.

HEMLOCK (*abies canadiensis*) is an important tanning material, both the bark and the wood being extensively used in America. The wood is now generally converted into extracts in factories built near the principal forests. Of late years, this extract has been imported into the United Kingdom in fairly large quantities, in order to produce a cheap red sole leather to compete with the American hemlock-tanned leather. It contains only about 25 per cent. of tannin, but its value is increased by its contents of insoluble non-tannins, which give weight and solidity to the leather. Hemlock really gives a strong, durable leather, but in America the practice of using artificial weighing materials, such as glucose and Epsom salts, with a reduced quantity of tanning material, has considerably lowered the value of this leather.

In addition to the materials described, there are several of minor importance which can only be briefly mentioned.

LARCH BARK is obtained from the tree *larix Europea*, which is found in Scotland and North Europe. It contains 10-12 per cent. of tannin, which gives a light colour and pleasant odour to leather. Scotch basils (sheep skins) are tanned with this bark.

BIRCH BARK, from the white birch, *betula alba*, is another aromatic tanning material. It contains only about 5 per cent. of tannin, and is, therefore, generally used with other tanning materials. It contains a tar which imparts an agreeable scent to the leather that protects it from the ravages of insects. In conjunction with willow bark (*salix arenaria*) it is used in the tanning process for the real Russia leather. An oil containing the scent can be extracted from the birch bark by dry distillation, and this extract is sometimes used during the dyeing process, in the manufacture of imitation Russia leather, which, however, only retains the scent for a few months, whereas the real Russia leather has a permanent odour.

CANAIGRE (*rumex hymenosepalum*) is the tuberous root of a dock plant indigenous to Mexico and the Southern States of America. It is fairly rich in tannin (25-30 per cent.) and yields a moderately firm leather. It contains too large a proportion of starch, however, and cannot be described as a really satisfactory tannin. Moreover, it is not harvested economically and the only way to make a satisfactory tannin of it is to convert it into extract and remove the starchy matters near the source of supply, if anyone dare take the risk of establishing a factory in Mexico.

BABLAH or BABOOL (*acacia arabica* or *acacia vera*) grows in India, Egypt, and the Sudan. The bark of the babool tree is one of the principal tanning materials used in India for hides, calf, and sheep skins, which are sent in large quantities to Great Britain in a rough-tanned state and dressed there. It contains 15-20 per cent. of tannin, which readily oxidises in the leather in contact with light, turning into a bright pink colour. It also seems to weaken the fibres of animal tissues, and, for that reason, babool-tanned leather was condemned by the Society of Arts Commission on Bookbinding.

The pods contain from 20-30 per cent. of tannin and give a mellow and plump leather similar to that produced by gambier. The bleaching of the material is troublesome, and it is probable that its use would be increased if the tannin were prepared in the form of extract.

Cutch is a crude extract made from the Indian tree *acacia catechu*. This is the real cutch, as distinguished from the mangrove "cutch." It is very rich in tannin (50-60 per cent.), but contains a large proportion of insoluble matter and is, therefore, very little used for tanning. It is well adapted for the dyeing of dark colours or black with mineral strikers, such as chrome and iron salts; but its chief use is for tanning fishermen's nets, which it renders waterproof.

Commercial tannic acid, used for medicinal purposes, is prepared from galls or excrescences on oak trees growing in Asia Minor. These galls are caused by an insect (*cynips*) puncturing the small branches and producing abnormal growth in the perforated parts. The acid is gallotannic, which, if used for making leather, would produce a soft, spongy, and nearly white leather. This tanning material is used a little by Near Eastern tanners, but the result is unsatisfactory.

Classification of Tanning Materials

Tanning materials are divided into two main classes: (1) Pyrogallol, (2) Catechol. The pyrogallol tannins give a bluish-black colour, and the catechol tannins a greenish-black, with iron salts. Bromine water does not precipitate pyrogallols, but causes a precipitate with catechols. Pyrogallols yield ellagic acid (called "bloom" in the trade), which improves the waterproof qualities of leather. On the other hand, catechols contain a large proportion of insoluble reds, or phlobaphenes, which are deposited between the fibres and thus give solidity to the leather. Pyrogallol tannins give a light coloured, soft leather, and can be used alone satisfactorily; but heavy leathers, such as sole and belting, need a blend of both kinds of tannin. The pyrogallol tannins include sumach, chestnut, myrobalans, divi-divi, oakwood, algarobilla, chestnut oak, willow, and galls. The catechols include quebracho, gambier, hemlock, mimosa or wattle, mangrove, larch, birch, canaigre, and cutch. Oak bark and valonia contain some of the properties of both classes of tannins.

There are sub-divisions of these two classes, arranged according to chemical tests, by which one tanning material can be distinguished from another.

Tanning Extracts

The manufacture of extracts from vegetable tanning materials has increased so rapidly of late years that the process of tanning has undergone radical changes; and, whereas the tanner was limited to three or four materials thirty years ago, he now has the choice of about twenty good materials. These tannins can be suitably blended to produce first-class leather. The processes in extract manufacture are few. The wood, bark, or fruit is broken up into small pieces and macerated in hot or cold water. The concentration of the liquid is done in vacuum, or in an evaporator. The latest method is to treat the tan liquor in a "triple-effect" evaporator (Fig. 4), the object of using three compartments being to economise in steam. This apparatus makes liquid extracts; where a powdered or crystal extract is required, the liquid is afterwards treated in a vacuum drying apparatus. Some extracts contain a lot of colouring matter and insoluble substances. To overcome this defect, they are clarified with blood albumen, sulphites, casein, or acetate of lead.

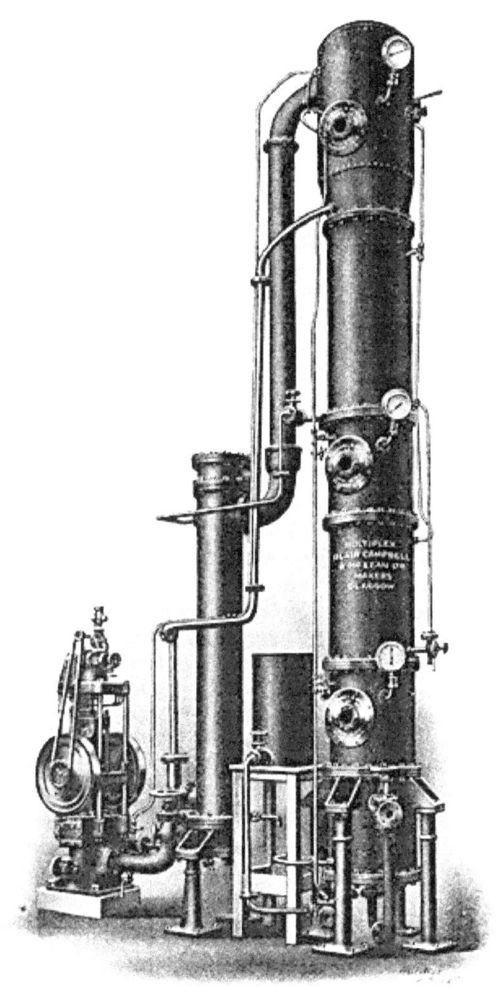

FIG. 4. —TRIPLE-EFFECT EVAPORATOR
(Blair, Campbell & McLean, Ltd.)

Synthetic Tannins

The discovery of a synthetic tannin, in 1911, by Dr. Stiasny, who was then an assistant in the Leather Industries Department of Leeds University, created a great deal of interest in the leather trade, and can certainly be regarded as a triumph of the application of chemistry to industry. It was thought at first that these tannins might play as important a part in the leather trade as the synthetic dye-stuffs have, but it is now generally believed that this will not be the case. Their use is likely to be as an aid to tanning, rather than as a complete tanning agent, although it has been found practicable to use them for one or two classes of light skins, where it is essential that the colour of the leather should be nearly white.

The original patent was taken out in September, 1911, in Austria, the native country of the inventor, but the patent rights have also been protected in other countries, while the manufacture and sale of the product passed into the hands of a large German dye firm, who have since taken out several patents for other synthetic tannins. The original tannin is produced by treating a sulphonated phenol with formaldehyde. A patent had been taken out several years before for the use of formaldehyde in tanning, but this expired early in 1911; many patents had also been granted for sulphonated phenol preparations, chiefly as disinfectants, but it was left to Dr. Stiasny to discover the value of combining the two chemicals by the process of condensation. The preparation, first known as "neradol," is now made in England under licence, but, since the war, its cost has been more than doubled, so that it is unlikely to replace natural tanning materials to any great extent.

Formaldehyde itself has certain properties which are harmful to leather, and it must be used with extreme caution and in small quantities to avoid these defects. It is used in the leather trade chiefly for keeping up the substance of hides during the tanning process, and thus causing a rapid absorption of tannin. At the beginning of the tanning process, the liquors are acidified, preferably with a weak organic acid, which causes the fibres of the hides to distend. It is at this stage that the formaldehyde is used. This method, which cannot improve, but may easily damage, the leather, is almost entirely confined to the Continent. Formaldehyde has a hardening and tanning effect on animal tissues, and leather treated by this process often has inferior wearing qualities.

In the case of the artificial tannin, this property of formaldehyde is to a large extent modified by the chemical reaction with a sulphonated phenol, the addition of which also increases its tanning effect; but, while the tannage is very rapid, especially in the case of light skins, leather produced solely by means of artificial tannin has a slight tendency to dryness after being in stock for some time.

No doubt, however, methods will be found to overcome initial difficulties, and various liquors will be prepared to meet different requirements. The question of price remains the deciding factor as to its use on an extensive scale, for, while it is so high, natural tanning materials will be preferred, except in a few special cases. According to the hide-powder method of tannin analysis, Neradol contains about 30 per cent. of tannin, but there are many natural tannin extracts containing nearly double the amount of tannin at nearly half the price of the artificial tannin; the latter, however, has a more rapid action and also produces a nearly white leather. Another advantage of Neradol is that it prevents drawn grain, so that, if raw hides be treated with a small quantity before tanning, stronger vegetable tan liquors may be safely used to hasten the process. In the manufacture of sole leather, for example, limed hides, after washing in water, may be suspended in a solution of Neradol containing 3 to 5 lb. per 100 gal. of water for twelve to twenty-four hours. This quantity produces a slight tanning effect, the hides are thoroughly delimed, and strong vegetable tan liquors may then be used to complete the tannage without the grain of the hide being drawn or dark in colour, as would be the case if the hides were not first treated with the artificial tannin.

Neradol is also said to be an effective bleaching agent for tanned leather in a 5 per cent. solution for a few hours, without any loss of weight.

This property may also be utilised in the production of chrome leather, where a whiter colour is required than that produced by the ordinary chrome tannage. For this purpose it may be used in a pickling liquor before the one-bath process, or in the second bath of the two-bath tannage.

For dressing wool and fur skins, the synthetic tannins are much superior to the alum and salt process.

CHAPTER IV LEATHER WORKING MACHINERY

When it is considered that the construction of machinery for the leather trade had barely started thirty years ago, the wonderful variety and utility of modern machines are remarkable, and it is a moot point whether engineering science has not played as great a part as, or even greater than, applied chemistry.

Excepting the bark mill, various kinds of tumblers, the fulling stocks, glazing and rolling machines, there were practically no efficient mechanical aids to lighten the exceedingly laborious operations incidental to leather manufacture two decades ago; but so many improvements have lately been made in the construction of machinery for practically every operation in the trade that most of the machines require very little skill to work them, and can be operated by intelligent youths after a few weeks' experience.

The change has been of great benefit to the health of the workers, for the continual stooping over beams and sloping tables, combined with the arduous nature of the work, was very injurious. The reputation that tanning had as a healthy occupation was due more to the work of the labourers than that of the skin workers. (The old-fashioned lime-yards and tan-yards were generally in the open, whereas modern tanneries are roofed.)

Leather trades machinery was not a success at first, probably because it was very difficult to get the necessary information from leather manufacturers. However, as the engineers gained more experience of the methods of leather-making, the defects were gradually remedied until it may be truly said that the machines now reach a high state of perfection. It was no uncommon thing for workmen to lose a finger or two in a machine, but such accidents are now rare, owing to improvements in the construction of the machines.

Most of the machines used in the leather trade are of the cylinder type, the raw skins or leather passing between two rollers, of which the upper one performs the operation while the lower one helps to draw the material through the machine. To prevent accidents and control the working of machines, a third roller is often used, which serves to "feed" the leather or skins to the working cylinders. Of this type of safety roller, the Seymour-Jones attachment to the shaving and buffing machine is of great importance.

Fig. 5

SHAVING CYLINDER

The operations of the tannery, which are performed by cylindrical machines, are dehairing, fleshing, scudding, samming, shaving, scouring, striking-out, setting, boarding, buffing, graining, printing, embossing, and blacking or colouring. The working cylinders usually vary according to the character of the operation, although one or two types may be used for at least three different operations.

Where cutting or paring is done, the working cylinder is fitted with brass blades, or steel blades backed with iron. The blades are spiral in some machines, and are so arranged that half of them converge to the left, and half to the right (Fig. 5). When in work, this type of cylinder not only performs the operation for which it is specially intended, but also stretches the leather outward, by reason of the arrangement of the blades or knives. The blades overlap one another to obviate marking, for if the blades met exactly at the centre they would make a line on the leather. Figure 6 shows another arrangement of knives for the process of buffing.

FIG. 6
BLADED CYLINDER FOR "BUFFING" LEATHER

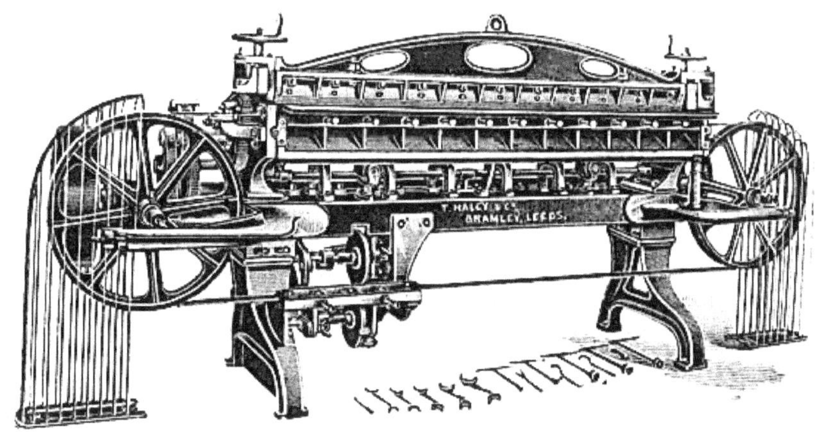

FIG. 7
BAND-KNIFE SPLITTING MACHINE

The most important machines outside the working cylinder type are the splitter, and the glazer. There are several kinds of splitting machines, but the band-knife machine (Fig. 7) is the most largely used. This is a veritable triumph of the engineer's art, for it is possible to make five or six layers, all about the same size, out of one hide, although leather is only split once or twice as a rule. Of course, sole, belting, and other thick leathers are not usually split. The invention of the belt-knife splitting machine revolutionised the leather trade, and there would undoubtedly have been a great shortage of leather without it. Formerly, all the levelling and reducing of substance was done by paring off quite small pieces with the shaving knife (Fig. 8), a difficult and laborious work. These parings were only suitable for pulping and compressing into leather board; but now the flesh splits removed by the machine can be curried, enamelled, printed, or rolled to make serviceable leathers, although, of course, not nearly so good in quality as the top or grain split. The main working part of the splitting machine is an endless steel knife which passes round two wheels placed at opposite ends of the machine. The leather is drawn to the knife through two rollers, of which the lower one is in sections to allow very thick parts of the hide to pass through the machine. It would need a large volume to describe in detail all the different machines used in the leather trade; the constructional details of only one machine can be given, and, in view of its importance, the shaver is selected. Reproductions of other machines will appear in succeeding chapters.

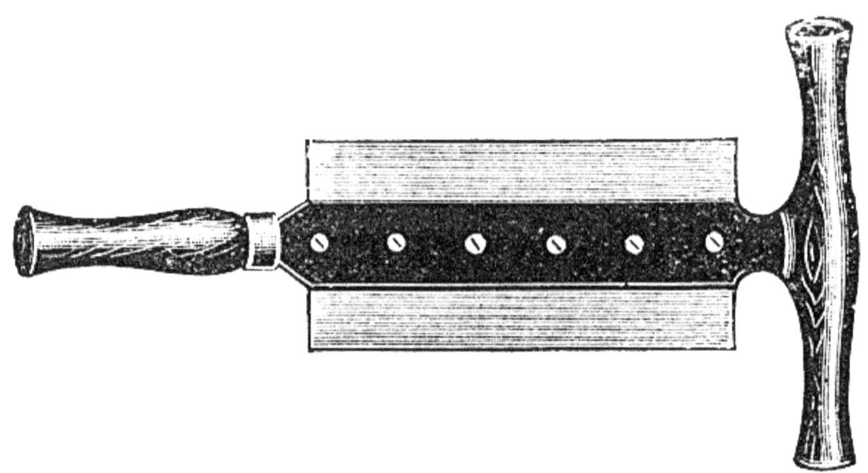

FIG. 8
SHAVING KNIFE

Nearly every leather trades' engineer constructs shaving machines, but the Howard-Smith is described here, not because it is the most popular (unfortunately there is a decided preference for low-priced machines), but because it is one of the best from an engineering point of view, and because several improvements are embodied in its construction.

FIG. 9
SHAVING LEATHER
(Old method)

This machine consists of nearly one hundred parts and each is made of the best material available. The advantage of this is obvious when the question of repairs is fully considered. The first Howard-Smith machine made has been running more than four years, and has not cost the owner a penny for repairs, beyond, of course, the expense of replacing the blades of the working cylinders; whereas it is no uncommon occurrence for a cheap machine to be thrown on the scrap heap after a few years' wear. It is always advisable, therefore, to buy machinery of the best grade.

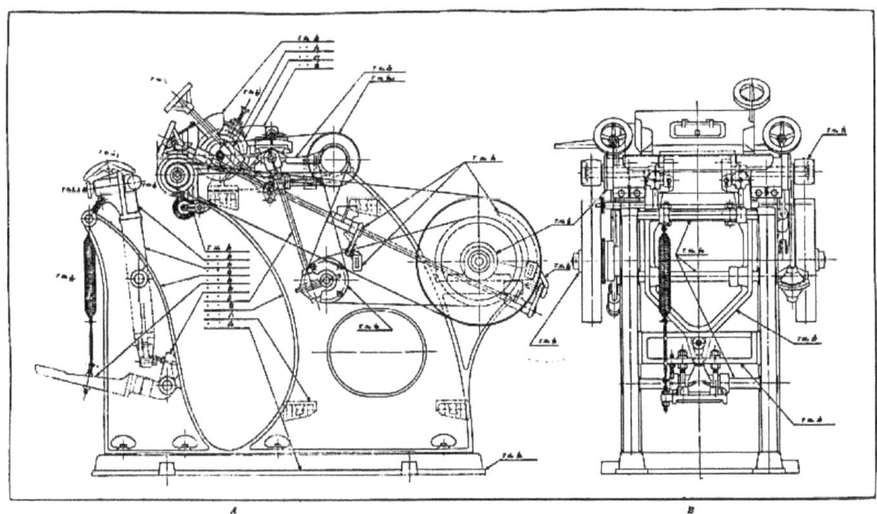

bet, pp. 56 & 57

Fig. 10

DRAWING OF SHAVING MACHINE

Figure 10 represents a drawing of the shaving machine, *A* being the side view, and *B* the front. The work of the draughtsman generally appears to the uninitiated to border on the miraculous; he is often the designer and architect of the machine, and his work is certainly interesting and skilful.

Many of the heavy parts, such as main castings, pedestals, etc., are made in the foundry, which may be part of the leather trades' engineer's works if he is in a large way of business. The finer parts, those which might be termed the fittings, are made in the turnery department; while the machine is assembled in the fitters' shop.

Figure 10 *A* shows the side, and 10 *B* the front construction of the shaving machine. The figures indicate, by following the arrows, the principal parts of the machine, which are shown in detail in sectional tracings. For example, *T.* 65, of which no working parts are shown in the diagram of the complete machine, is reproduced in detail in a separate drawing shown in Figure 11. Each part of the machine is numbered and entered in a stock-book.

In describing the principal parts indicated in Figure 10, it will give an idea of the assembling of the machine if a beginning be made with the main iron castings. These comprise the main bed (64), two side frames (62), and the front frame (58). The side frames are strengthened by the ribs which form the edge, and which are about three times as thick as the body of the casting. The object of the front frame is to support the foot lever (59), the rocking frame (57) carrying the rubber roll (79), and the wooden roof (75) over which the leather is passed. The spring (76) pulls back the rocking frame (57) when relieved by the operator removing his foot from the lever (59). The long spring (77) lifts up the foot lever (59) when the latter is released.

The pullies (73) are connected with the knife cylinder which shaves the leather. The cylinder is obscured by the wheel-guard (65) and is, therefore, shown separately. This cylinder is comprised of a shaped piece of steel (turned out of solid metal bars of 4-3/4 in. diameter) into which spiral steel blades are caulked with copper or brass. When turned, the body of the cylinder is 4-5/8 in. in diameter, but the parts forming the bearings are reduced to 1-1/2 in. The number of blades is twelve, fourteen, or sixteen, according to the kind of leather shaved, and to the choice of the operator.

It is interesting to note that these blades are now being made in Sheffield, although, before the war, they had to be imported. The knife guard (65), shown in detail in Figure 11, is an ingenious contrivance which prevents the operator's hands being drawn into the machine. It consists of an automatic shutter worked by a steel chain from the foot lever. Figure 11 *a* represents the shutter closed down on the knife with the rubber roll, on which the leather is carried to the knife, at a safe distance from the shutters. Fig. 11 *b* shows the position when the machine is shaving the leather, the guard being clear and the rubber roll engaged with the knife.

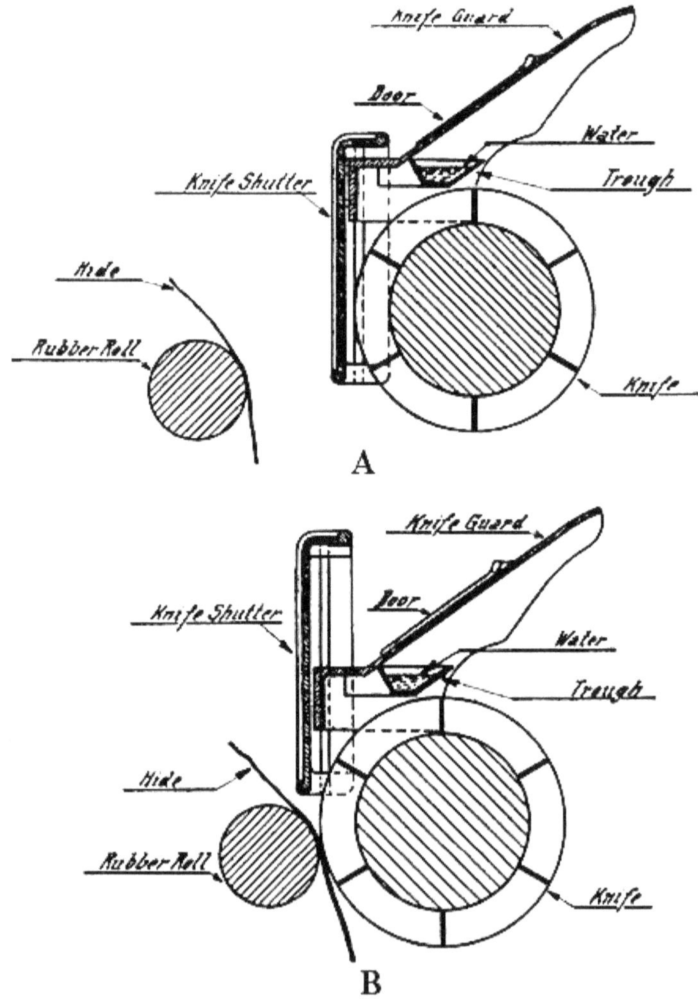

Fig. 11.

In order to sharpen the blades of the cylinder, a carborundum wheel is fixed in close proximity, its position being indicated in the drawing by the wheel cover (67). A bracket for feeding the wheel to the blades when grinding them is shown at 66. When grinding the blades, the saddle (68) carries the wheel backwards and forwards across them. A special feature of the saddle in this particular machine is the double-thread screw, one a right hand, and the other a left hand. The saddle (68) is actuated by a "swimmer," as the makers term it, which engages, say, first the right-hand thread; when the saddle has travelled to the end of its movement the "swimmer" automatically enters the left-hand thread, and the saddle is rotated in the opposite direction. The "swimmer" can be disengaged instantaneously. A brush (55) is fixed near the cylinder to remove any leather shavings adhering to the blades. It also acts to some extent as a fan, and, by creating a current of air, carries the leather dust away from the operator. A trough is filled with water to catch the dust from the carborundum wheel, while the knives are being ground. The trough should be cleared out and refilled with clean water from time to time. It is essential that no dust from the grinding wheel comes into contact with vegetable tanned leather required in a natural or colour finish, otherwise it will cause iron stains, which are difficult to remove without damaging the leather. For this reason, the knives should not be ground while this class of leather is being shaved.

An important detail of the machine under description is a trueing device. Knives are often roughened owing to the carborundum wheel wearing irregularly. The trueing device keeps the wheel perfectly true by means of a diamond held in the end of a screw (78). Another ingenious arrangement (patented) is a spring (79a) placed at the back of the rubber roll (79), which enables the roll to spring back when the leather, or any part of it, is too thick for the cutting cylinder.

A unique advantage of the Howard-Smith machine is that it is ball-bearing throughout. The main driving shaft revolves on four massive ball-bearings in case (71). The pullies are firmly fixed to the driving shaft with keys or feathers. Afterwards the pullies are machined, so that the whole shaft with its pullies is perfectly balanced, and the machine runs smoothly without vibration.

The bladed cylinder is likewise mounted on four ball-bearings. The intermediate driving shaft (70), which is mounted on two ball-bearings, is connected with a large drum shaft (70a) which, in its turn, sets the carborundum wheel in motion.

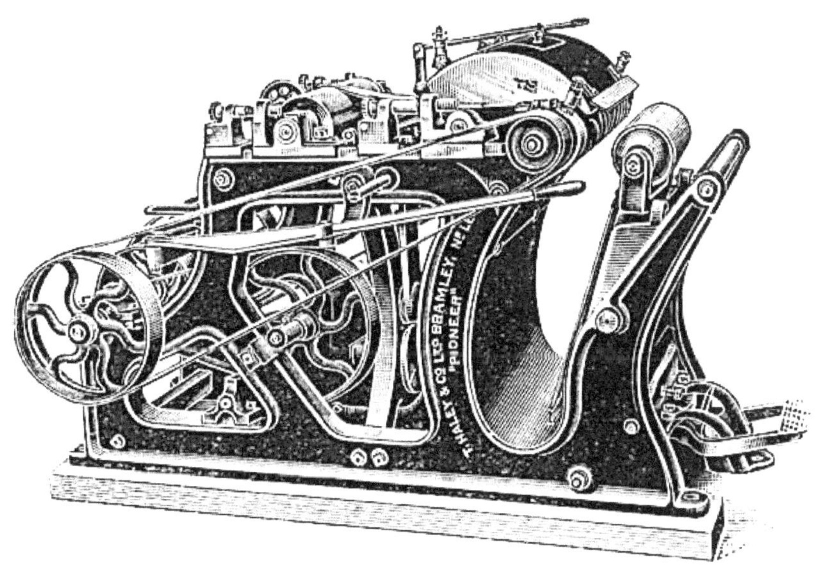

FIG. 12
SHAVING-MACHINE

(Haley)
Fig. 12 represents another make of shaving machine.

CHAPTER V PREPARATION OF HIDES AND SKINS FOR TANNING

Before beginning a description of manufacturing processes, a precise definition of leather may be given. Laymen usually describe leather as "hides tanned with bark," Since the introduction of modern processes, however, this is only partly true. In any case, the definition is very broad.

The primary objects of treating raw hides and skins to produce leather is to make them imputrescible and impart various degrees of pliability. These qualities are essential, but the simpler the methods used to attain them, the greater the strength of the leather produced.

The number of materials that will produce leather is legion. Whereas oak bark was almost exclusively used for tanning until the last century, there are now at least twenty useful vegetable tanning materials. The active ingredient of all of these materials is tannin, a colloidal or uncrystallisable substance. Correctly speaking, the term "tanning," used to designate the process of converting hides into leather, should be confined to the use of vegetable tannins; unfortunately, the trade has largely adopted the word in many other processes of making leather. For example, large quantities of leather are produced by the use of minerals, and especially of chrome salts; where the latter is used, the leather is said to be "chrome-tanned," although "chromed" would be a more accurate definition. One mineral process of making leather, namely, that involving the use of alum, or alumina sulphate, and salt, is technically described as "tawing," The conversion of skins into leather by the use of oxidised oil is known as "chamoising," imitation chamois leather being made by that process. Nearly every mineral has the property of converting skins into leather, though most of them are of little practical value. The most successful are the chrome salts, and alum and salt. The use of iron salts would be by far the cheapest process, if means could be found whereby they could be successfully used. Sixty years ago, a chemist named Knapp experimented with iron salts, but failed to produce satisfactory leather. Patents were taken out in Austria in the early part of 1914 for the use of iron salts in tanning, while a patent of more recent date covers the use of iron salts in combination with chrome salts. Neither of these appears to be of much practical value. The cheapest and most stable iron salts, the sulphate and chloride, have strongly acidic properties, and, therefore, have a somewhat destructive and hardening effect on animal fibres. The iron salt that might convert skins into leather is the carbonate, which is difficult to prepare cheaply enough for commercial purposes, though it is used medicinally. A basic iron salt might also be useful, but iron tannages would only be suitable for black leather. Oils and fats also have leather-making properties, fish oils being used for the manufacture of "chamois" and antelope leather. There are other methods of producing leather which are not used on a large scale, but sufficient examples have been given to show that an exact definition of leather cannot be summed up in one or two words. There are now many kinds of leather produced by varying methods, and each class requires its own definition. Broadly speaking, however, leather is an imputrescible material produced from the raw skins of animals, chiefly of cattle, sheep, and goats, by treating them with tannins extracted from the barks, wood, fruit, or leaves of trees; or with chemicals (chiefly chrome salts, or alum and common salt); or with oils and fats.

The preliminary processes are of great importance, as they determine to a large extent the character of the finished leather. Mistakes made in the early processes can never be effectually remedied.

The first operation is technically known as soaking, and its object is to cleanse the hides or skins thoroughly. This is quite simple in the case of raw hides received direct from the slaughterhouse, as it is merely a question of soaking them in clean, soft water for a few hours. If the only water available is hard, 1/2 lb. of borax should be added for every 100 lb. of raw hides. Borax is useful in any case, as it is a splendid cleanser and a very useful chemical in the tannery. Most of the hides used in the United Kingdom, however, are wet-salted (*i.e.*, salted in the wet state), as it has become customary for most butchers to send hides and skins to the auction markets in all the principal towns, where they are offered for sale every week. It is still a debatable point among tanners as to whether it is better to buy hides direct from the butcher or through these markets. It is certainly a great advantage to put hides into work quickly (although not before they are quite cool), as time is saved in the soaking process, and there is practically no loss of gelatinous matter. On the other hand, the tanner is able to buy just the selection of hides that he wants from the auction markets. Under this arrangement, several days must elapse before the tanner receives them, and it is, therefore, absolutely necessary to preserve them, otherwise they begin to decompose quickly. The first sign of decay is the slipping of the hair, which, in that condition, may be pulled out of its roots quite easily. Micro-organisms multiply rapidly in the gelatine of the hide, the grain comes away, and decomposition sets in so quickly that, in a few days after the removal of the hide from the carcase, it may lose nearly half its value for tanning purposes if it has not been preserved by salting or by drying rapidly in the shade in a current of air. Salted hides need a more prolonged soaking than fresh hides, as it is essential that all trace of salt be removed before the next process, otherwise the finished leather may be flat, and poor in quality. Usually, two days' soaking in several changes of water is necessary. For the soaking process, fresh or salted hides and skins are either soaked in square, cement-lined, brick pits, or in wooden vats filled with clean, cold water. A good system is to put a pack of skins in one huge tank filled with clean water and leave them in soak overnight before transferring them to the ordinary pits. Each pit will take 50 hides, or 10 dozen calf skins, or 20 dozen goat skins. Tanners designate as a "pack" each lot of hides or skins they work through, irrespective of the quantity.

Fig. 13
DRUM TUMBLER

Fig. 14

FALLER STOCKS

Besides salting them, there are other ways of curing hides and skins, and a large proportion is simply dried or dry-salted, the salt in the latter method being applied while the hides are moist. Dry hides, whether "flint" (i.e., simply dried) or salted, require special treatment to make them soft and pliable, without which it would be impossible to convert them into leather. Soaking in plain water is insufficient, as it would need too much time, during which there would be a great loss of gelatine. The use of chemicals and mechanical motion are required; sometimes chemicals alone will thoroughly soften the hides, but this is not often the case. Both alkalies and acids may be used for softening dried hides, and it is difficult to say which gives the better result, although the former are frequently used, mainly because treatment with acids is a comparatively recent innovation. Both kinds are effective, but the use of acids retards the loosening of the hair, although it has been proved experimentally that acid-softened hides give a slightly improved yield of leather compared with the effect of the alkaline process —a noteworthy advantage where the finished leather is to be sold by weight. The acid generally used-formic-has antiseptic properties, and can have no harmful effect on animal tissues, as is generally the case where mineral acids, especially sulphuric, are used. Sulphurous acid is also said to be a good softening agent for hides, but it is rarely used. The most satisfactory alkalies are sulphide of sodium (crystallised or concentrated) and caustic soda, and of these two, the sulphide is preferred in nine cases out of ten. The quantities used vary according to the condition of the hides, but the average is about 1 lb. of caustic soda, or 1 lb. of concentrated sulphide of sodium (65 per cent.), or 2 lb. of crystallised sulphide of sodium (30 per cent.) for every 100 gal. of water. Of formic acid, 1 lb. is sufficient for 100 gal. of water. It is possible to soften hides by these means without mechanical acid, but the time is considerably shortened by "drumming" the hides, *i.e.*, placing them in a round or, preferably, a square tumbler fitted inside with shelves or staves (Fig. 13). The drum is rotated mechanically for a few hours, during which time the hides are thoroughly kneaded and softened by the alkali. Tanners often use a machine known as the "faller stocks" (Fig. 14), which kneads the hides very thoroughly, though somewhat drastically. The drum method is preferable, providing the hides can be suitably softened. An old method, and one that is used now by some of the small firms, is to "break over" (*i.e.*, vigorously scrape) the hides with a curved blunt knife fitted into two wooden handles. For this manual operation, the hide is placed, flesh side up, over the tanner's beam (Fig. 15) and is then scraped with the knife.

FIG. 15

TANNER'S BEAM

Another old method, which has not yet disappeared, is to make use of stale soak liquors, which, although efficient for softening purposes, cause a great loss of hide substance owing to the active growth of bacteria, which are developed as a result of the water becoming foul and putrid with dirt, blood, and dissolved gelatinous matter. This method of soaking is always dangerous, apart from the great loss of gelatine, for the thin grain (hyaline layer) is liable to be eaten away in patches, a defect which greatly reduces the value of leather.

Dried hides are not only difficult to treat successfully in the different processes of making them into leather, but they are also of highly speculative value, although they are well preserved when completely dry. It sometimes happens, however, that the drying is imperfect; it may, for example, have been so rapid that the exterior of both sides is thoroughly dried before the air is able to penetrate into the centre. The result is that the interior of the hide putrefies, but there may be no indication of this until the hides are soaked and softened, when they may fall to pieces and are only saleable to glue makers. Again, the hides may be dried in the hot sun and be badly blistered, with the same result as regards their value for leather. If the hides are dried in too high a temperature, they become horny and rarely make satisfactory leather owing to the difficulty of softening them. It is estimated that quite 10 per cent. of the dried hides are improperly cured and, therefore, useless for making into satisfactory leather.

Apart from the commercial risk in buying dry hides, their import, especially from Russia and China, is a source of danger in conveying the disease of anthrax to workmen. It has been conclusively proved that dried hides are much more liable than wet-salted hides to cause infection.

So far, only one country, the United States of America, has taken steps to prevent the importation of the disease of anthrax, although most countries have issued regulations in regard to the precaution to be taken to avoid infection by anthrax in those factories where imported hides, wool, hair, and bones are treated. It would seem that the most rational method would be to disinfect the hides before they are shipped, as it certainly appears to be unwise to import any form of disease; unfortunately, the first regulations issued by the American Government proved to be impracticable, as the suggested method had the effect of lowering the quality of the hides, and making the preliminary operations troublesome. Their second scheme, consisting of baling a certain number of hides in canvas disinfected with a 0.02 per cent. solution of mercuric chloride, is more satisfactory, for, although it may not sterilise all the anthrax spores inside the bale, it should prevent them reaching other goods. This Government order only applies to hides, skins, hair, and wool coming from countries where anthrax is known to be prevalent.

The disease of anthrax is generally contracted by workers through sores or cuts in the hand; the bacilli multiply rapidly in contact with the blood, and the first sign of disease is usually shown by a red swelling or pimple in the neck. If treated at this stage by anti-anthrax serum a cure is often effected, but if treatment is delayed the disease quickly proves fatal, the patient dying in awful agony. The germs of the disease may also be swallowed and the disease develop internally, but cases of this kind are rare.

Besides the danger to workers, there is the risk of cattle being infected. The effluent from tanneries where anthrax-infected skins are treated contains millions of bacilli, and it is doubtful if the latter are sterilised even when the effluents are precipitated and aërated before they are run into streams or municipal sewers. In any case, the sediment may be infected, and this ultimately finds its way to the land.

Until the various European Governments insist on imported hides from anthrax-infected areas being sterilised before shipment, the use of a disinfectant such as lysol or a similar cresylic compound, or bichloride of mercury, seems imperative in the first process of soaking. The use of these disinfectants would make the waste liquors fit for discharge into sewers or streams.

The English Public Health and River Pollution Acts have had a great effect in improving the hygiene of the tannery, although leather manufacturers have not welcomed them, as, in some cases, they have meant considerable expense in providing settling tanks for the treatment of waste liquors. The Public Health Act gives power to any town corporation to declare as offensive trades such businesses as tanning, hide and skin merchanting, fellmongering, tallow melting, etc., and several boroughs have taken advantage of this law. In such cases, anyone desiring to set up business in these trades must apply to the Town Council, who may or may not give their consent; in fact, a few applications to establish these businesses have lately been refused.

While the curing of wet hides with salt or in brine is more satisfactory than drying them, the use of ordinary salt is not an ideal method, as 10 per cent. brine dissolves hide substance. The recent introduction of a pure dry salt (99-98 per cent.) and of a sterilised salt for commercial purposes has to a large extent removed the objections to ordinary salt. Dry sulphate of soda is also a satisfactory cure. It may be that, as hygienic conditions are further advanced in the various industries, a suitable disinfectant will have to be used for all hides, in addition to the salt, except where the hides are sent direct to the tannery from the slaughterhouse.

The cure of hides in hot countries, especially where cheap salt is unavailable, is often unsatisfactory. A method of obviating this difficulty has been found in China, where, in one or two of the principal towns, hides and skins are preserved by freezing them in cold-storage. Although this process stiffens the hides, it is said to be fairly satisfactory if they are allowed to soften naturally before soaking them. If submitted to rough treatment before the stiffness relaxes, there is a great danger of the hide fibres being ruptured. Freezing removes the difficulty of softening which is experienced in treating dried hides, while it preserves the hide substance.

After the operation of soaking, hides and skins are ready to be treated for the removal of the hair. There are several ways of loosening the hair sheaths, but most of them consist of treating the hides in a solution of a caustic alkali. The use of a solution of common lime was practically universal until a few years ago, but nowadays sulphide of sodium, red arsenic sulphide (realgar), and caustic soda are also used, generally in admixture with the lime. Another process consists in sweating the hides in a heated room, preferably a damp cellar, where rapid decomposition of the hides soon loosens the hair.

This method is rarely used in England, but a few American tanners seem to prefer it for certain classes of hides. In the American process, the hides are first soaked, and then cut in half down the back, forming what are known as sides. Dry hides are subjected to the usual mechanical operations in the faller stocks, in which they are kneaded by two large hammers (Fig. 14), or they are drummed in the tumbler (Fig. 13). After the sides are thoroughly softened and drained, they are transferred to the sweat pit, which is, preferably, a dark underground chamber. The stock requires very careful attention as the process is risky. The temperature should never exceed 75° F., otherwise the hides may be irretrievably ruined. The process may take from one to four days, according to the varying conditions of the hides and of the weather. The loss of nitrogenous matter gives rise to the development of a strong odour of ammonia, which is sometimes even too pungent for the workmen. When the hair is judged to be sufficiently loose, the sides are washed in cold water and put in the stocks again for about ten minutes, when all the hair will be removed; or the hair may be scraped off in the unhairing machine. This method is not useful for sole leather, as it causes too great a loss of gelatine, but it saves time in the production of sides intended for boot upper leather, which is usually sold by measurement (superficial area).

A dehairing process has lately been invented and patented, however, which may supersede all of the methods just described. This process consists in treating the hides with various enzymes which loosen the hair so effectively that it can be removed more easily than the hair of a limed hide. The fine, short hairs underneath are also removed, whereas by the lime method a further process is needed to get rid of these hairs. The only drawback to its use is that the inventor has not yet been able to produce a material cheap enough to place on the market, but as soon as this difficulty is overcome the enzyme method may become fairly general. Neither the hair nor the gelatine of the hide can be damaged by this method.

Fig. 16
LIME YARD
("Dri-ped" Tannery)

The usual method of liming is carried out in brick pits of square or rectangular shape with a sloping front on which the hides or skins can be piled to drain (Fig. 16). There is a great variation in the quality of lime, and in all cases it should be tested for the available percentage of caustic lime. A good sample should contain between 70 and 80 per cent. of pure lime. Buxton lime, which can be obtained in powdered form, is particularly suitable for the tannery. The ordinary lime is preferable to the chalk lime, as it is usually stronger, though it sometimes contains more impurities. Gas lime is the poorest of all. Lime should be stored in a dark place, otherwise the outside of the heap carbonates quickly, forming chalk (Ca O + CO$_2$ = Ca CO$_3$) which is of no use for the liming process.

To prepare the lime for the pits it is slaked (*i.e.*, formed into a paste with water. All the lumps should be reduced to paste in order to avoid lime burns, which are caused by direct contact of the hides with pieces of unslaked lime. A certain quantity of the paste is then added to the water or old lime liquor in the pit, and the liquor is well plunged up to hasten solution and diffusion of the lime. A long wooden pole, with a flat block of wood attached, is used for this purpose and also for pressing down the hides under the surface of the liquor.

Two methods of liming are in vogue: (1) the single-pit system, and (2) the three-pit system; but the latter is the better method, as it is more easily controlled, and causes less loss of gelatine than the former. In this system the liquor is strengthened with fresh lime for each pack of skins. Its great fault is that the pit is only cleared out at long intervals in order to take advantage of the mellowness of used lime liquors; hence, there is frequently large accumulation of insoluble limestone and other sediment from the lime, in addition to a quantity of dissolved gelatine, which rapidly accumulates putrefactive bacteria. When the pit is cleared out the process of liming is disturbed for a time, as fresh lime liquors are not beneficial to hides and skins, and the loosening of the hair is delayed. On the other hand, the three-pit system permits liquors of uniform strength, and the process is continued without interruption. Each new pack is first placed in the oldest of the three liquors, which is then cleared out, and a new liquor prepared. From the weakest pit the hides pass to a stronger liquor, and the process is finished in the third pit, which should contain a new lime liquor. The mellow liquors, being charged with bacteria, facilitate the loosening of the hair, while the third liquor, consisting of fresh lime, serves to swell the fibres of the hide, by means of which the flesh is more effectually removed. The lime also forms a soap with the natural grease of the hide; this grease can therefore be removed. In some cases, however, especially in the cattle fed up for Christmas, the hides contain a larger quantity of fat than the alkali of the lime liquor can convert into a soap, and the surplus grease is frequently seen in the finished leather, as it is difficult to remove in later processes. A solution of hyposulphite of soda, or lactic acid, given just before the process of tanning is said to remove the grease, although a slight loss results in the case of those leathers sold by weight. The objection to natural grease in leather can be understood where the latter is intended for colours, but in the case of sole leather it ought not to be a disadvantage, yet, owing merely to the darker appearance of the leather where the grease reaches the grain, its selling value is reduced by 2d. or 3d. per lb. The strange part is that the grain of this sole leather, when made into boots, is buffed on an emery wheel, then sometimes coloured with a paint, and finally sold in boots at the same price as leather free from grease and regular in colour.

The liming process in pits takes from six days to a month, according to the character of the leather required. Light calf skins may be ready for unhairing within a week, while hides intended to be finished for "raw hide leather" may be left in the pits quite a month, the object being to distend and harden the fibres. Lamb skins intended for parchment, and small calf skins for vellum, are also subjected to prolonged liming. Between these extremes, there are several stages in the process which have varying effects on the character of the finished leather. In fact, it is a tanner's dictum that leather is made or marred in the lime liquor, though this, of course, only applies to a certain extent. Generally, however, the heavier the hides, the longer the liming required. Fortunately, the limited solubility of the lime in water affords a wide margin of safety in working, and the only danger to guard against is the too prolonged use of old liquors, which are readily detected by the strong odour of ammonia. One important property of lime is its lower solubility in hot than in cold water.

Lime by itself does not readily attack the hair bulbs, and the slowness of the process has led to the introduction of other chemicals, generally for use in conjunction with lime. The principal of these are sulphide of sodium and red arsenic. Mixtures of sulphide of sodium and lime, or red arsenic and lime are now largely used, the former for hides, calf, and sheep skins, and the latter for goat and kid skins. Both sulphide of sodium and arsenic dissolve keratinous matters (horns, hair, etc.) and workmen should, therefore, be provided with rubber gloves to prevent the loss of their finger nails. Sulphides naturally lower the commercial value of the hair removed and, if used alone, destroy it. In admixture, however, the hair has some value, although it is not so good as that removed by the use of pure lime. Against this, however, there is a great saving of time and less loss of hide substance and, therefore, increased weight of leather. Sulphide of sodium is prepared in crystallised or concentrated form; the former, about 30 per cent. strength, is preferred in Great Britain, while the latter —65 per cent. strength-is prepared for export, the main object being to save the cost of transit of 35 per cent. of water. About thirty different sulphide salts may be used, but the sodium and arsenic disulphides are the best, as it has been shown that the most rapid loosening of the hair occurs where the quantities of sulphur and alkali are nearly the same. There are two arsenic salts used in the trade, namely, realgar, or red sulphide of arsenic ($As_2 S_2$) and orpiment, or the yellow sulphide ($As_2 S_3$), but the former is often preferred as it is said to give better results than the latter. In practice, the proportion of arsenic used is 1 part in 20 parts of lime, although it naturally varies a little according to the class of skin under treatment. Sulphide of sodium is used in the proportion of 1 part to 10 of lime, or, if concentrated sulphide be used, 1 in 20. The quantities of lime, or lime and sulphide, used are estimated on the weight of the raw hides. For hides intended for sole leather, 5 per cent. of lime on the weight of hides is ample, while a little more may be used for hides intended for dressing leather (*i.e.*, leather which has to be dressed or finished with a certain degree of flexibility for bags, boot uppers, etc.). When a mixture of lime and sulphide is used, 3 per cent. and 0.3 per cent. respectively is a satisfactory quantity. The action of this mixture on hides is complex and has not yet been definitely ascertained, but it is thought that the calcium sulphydrate formed by the chemical reaction between sulphide of sodium and calcium hydrate (slaked lime) is the active principle.

In the pit method of liming, it is essential that the liquors be frequently plunged, while the hides should be taken out ("hauled"), piled to drain for a few hours, and put back again ("set"), or transferred to another pit. Although lime is more soluble in cold than in warm water, it is found in practice that the process may be stopped or considerably retarded in very cold weather, and the activity of the liquors is increased by the application of waste steam (conveyed through iron pipes from the boiler).

Sulphide of sodium and lime are sometimes made into a thin paste, which is applied to the hair side of hides and skins with a mop or fibre brush. The hides are then folded down the back with the flesh sides out; other hides are similarly treated and placed in a pile. This saves a great amount of labour in pitting, and, if the paste is fairly strong, consisting of 2 to 2-1/2 per cent. sulphide, the hair can be removed after a few hours.

With so many depilatories available, it is not surprising that several patents have been granted and numerous suggestions made with the object of trying to improve on the old process of liming. While there may be some objections to lime, it has a few advantages which are lacking in other depilatories. These advantages are not perfectly understood theoretically, but the tanner recognises them in practice. Hence, there are very few tanneries where lime is not used at all, and the only progress that seems to have been made in the process of liming consists in the admixture of sulphide of sodium or arsenic to hasten the process, reduce the loss of gelatine, and, in the case of arsenic, to improve the fineness of the grain of skins for boot upper and glove leathers.

One patented method consisted in forming the calcium hydrate within the hide by treating it with a 1 per cent. solution of caustic soda and then with a 1-1/2 per cent. solution of calcium chloride, the reaction of these two chemicals forming calcium hydrate (lime) and sodium chloride (salt). This method, however, does not loosen the hair at all and has to be supplemented by soaking the hides in putrid water. It is a good method of liming hides or skins dressed in the hair, as it opens up the fibres without weakening the hair roots and prepares the hides in a suitable condition for tanning.

Another method consists in mixing a small quantity of soda ash with the lime, thereby hastening the process by increasing the alkalinity of the liquor.

A somewhat complicated method was introduced a few years ago, but, although it seemed advantageous from a chemical point of view, it has not proved successful in practice so far as is known, probably because of its expense. In consisted of four distinct processes. The hides were first mopped on the hair side with a thin paste of lime and arsenic, and dehaired after twenty-four hours. In the second process, they were treated in a drum for twenty-four hours with a solution of sodium sulphide, they were then drummed for twenty-four hours in a solution of hyposulphite of soda, and finally placed in a vat or pit containing a solution of lime and a little arsenic for two to five days. After washing, etc., they were ready for tanning. The sulphide of sodium swelled the hides or skins by distending the fibres, and the natural fat is converted into a soluble soap. The hyposulphite arrests the action of the sulphide and acts as an antiseptic.

In modern yards it is a growing practice to use mechanical power to keep the hides in motion, instead of handling them. The hides are attached to poles joined to a strong cross beam, which, in its turn, is connected by stout iron rods with the main pullies and shafting. The installation is expensive, but it saves an enormous amount of manual labour and time, while ensuring uniform treatment. This method is not so much used for liming as for the tanning process.

After loosening the hair and opening up the fibres, the next operation is dehairing or depilation, or, as it is generally described in the trade, "unhairing." The hair must slip quite easily before beginning this operation, otherwise a number of them will be left in the hide and will be difficult, or almost impossible, to remove later on if the hides are being made into sole leather. These hairs present an unsightly appearance and lower the value of the leather. Depilation may be done by hand or machine; but the latter method is rapidly superseding the former, as it is in nearly every other process of leather manufacture.

In the manual process, the hair is removed by scraping it off in a downward direction with a blunt, convex-shaped knife, fitted into two wooden handles (Fig. 17), the hides being placed on a sloping convex beam (Fig. 15) supported by a trestle. A series of grooves under the beam permits it to be placed at any angle. The beam (different from that used by curriers) may be of wood, iron, steel, or zinc-covered wood.

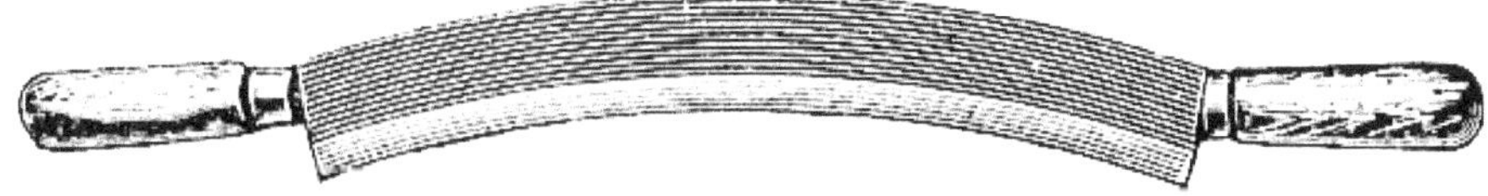

FIG. 17

DEHAIRING KNIFE

There are several types of unhairing machines, of which the Leidgen more nearly approaches hand work than any other. The skins are placed on a soft bed of felt, and the working roller, fitted with spiral knives, is brought into contact with the hide and scrapes off the hair.

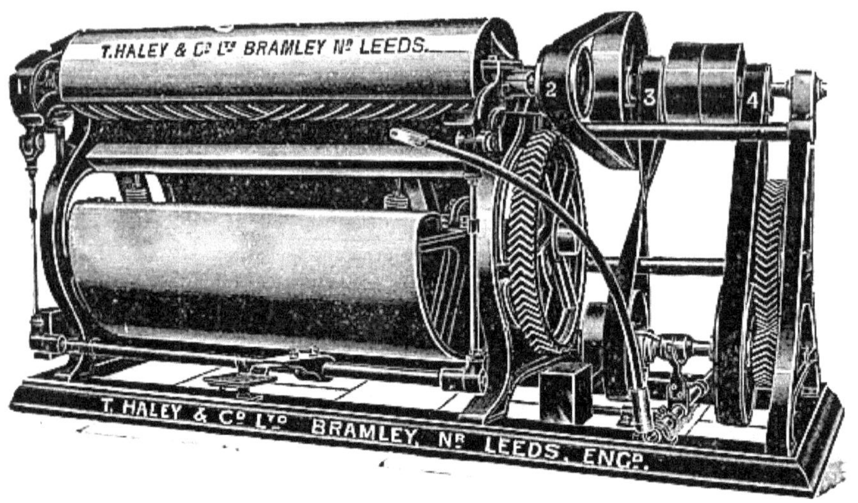

Fig. 18

DEHAIRING AND FLESHING MACHINE

The type of machine often used, however, is shown in Figure 18; the working part is a long spindle fitted with helical knives. The advantages of this machine are its large output and its use for other operations by simply changing the working roller. The blades must be blunt for dehairing, but sharpened blades are needed for fleshing.

If hides intended for sole leather are being dehaired, the short hairs which are not removed by the dehairing knife are carefully scraped off with a sharp knife. Other kinds of hides and skins are freed from short hairs in a later operation.

When the hides are dehaired, they are sometimes submitted at once to the next operation of fleshing, which, as its name implies, consists in removing loose flesh and fat from the "flesh" side, that is, the side near the carcase. The extent to which this operation is carried out depends on the quality of the finished leather. Naturally, the more flesh left on the greater the weight, particularly as loose flesh will absorb a large quantity of tannin, and, unfortunately, of adulterants which are frequently used for weighting common leathers. The flesh ought to be removed in all cases, for the loose flesh forms very poor and spongy leather. Where hides and skins are tanned and then dried for sale to leather dressers and finishers, there is often the tendency to leave far too much loose flesh on them, with the object of producing as much weight of leather as possible. From the point of view of economy, this is a mistake, for the loose flesh must be removed during the dressing process, whereas, if it had been taken off at first, both material and time would have been saved in the process of tanning.

If the fleshing is not done directly after dehairing, the hides or skins should be placed in a weak lime liquor, and this method is to be recommended. The great point to be observed is to keep the limed hides, both before and after dehairing, away from contact with the air, as the chemical action of the carbonic acid on lime results in the formation of chalk, which tends to harden the hides and to roughen the grain, so that it is likely to be scratched in later operations. Where the hides are intended for sole leather, and not treated with an acid before entering the tanning liquors, the presence of chalk would lead to an uneven colouring of the leather.

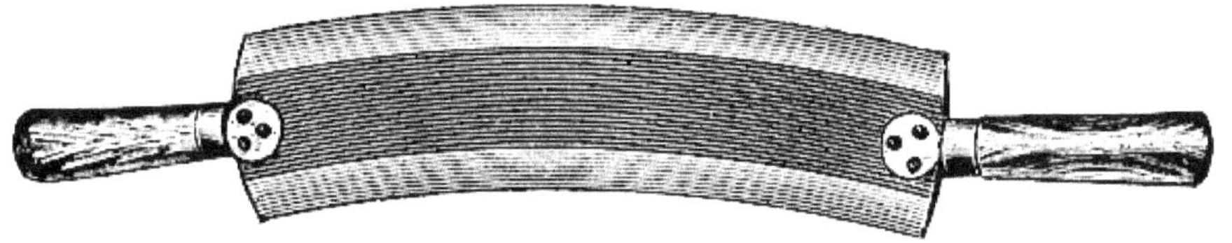

Fleshing by hand demands great skill. The knife used (Fig. 19) is similar to the unhairing knife, except that it has two edges. The cutting is done with the convex edge, which has to be kept very sharp. The concave edge need not be sharp, its use being limited to scraping off loose particles of flesh, while the parts not removed by this means are cut off with the sharp edge. The knife is held slantingly, with the blade almost parallel with the beam. The strokes should be short and in a semicircular direction, otherwise it is difficult to avoid cutting the skins. This manual operation is now largely superseded by machinery, and will, no doubt, soon be obsolete. The early types of fleshing machines were not a success, but the modern machine is very effective. There are several makes on the market, but in most cases the working tool is of similar construction and consists of a long cylinder to which spiral knives are fixed. (Fig. 18.) Half of these blades converge to the left and half to the right, the object being not only to cut away the flesh but also to stretch the hides outward, thus ensuring an evenly cut surface. The fleshings and useless pieces of skin are kept in a weak lime liquor until there is a sufficient quantity to send to the glue maker; although in some of the larger tanneries this offal, technically termed "spetches," or glue pieces, is converted into glue on the premises. In hot weather, a large accumulation of fleshings is liable to putrefaction, despite the use of plenty of lime water. While lime certainly arrests putrefaction of gelatinous matter for a time, decomposition afterwards sets in and serious damage may be done. To avoid this, it has been a common practice in Germany to use formaldehyde, but, while this acts as a preservative, it hardens animal tissues, and has a tanning effect, with the result that the pieces are rendered insoluble and cannot, of course, be reduced to a liquid gelatine by boiling. Glue makers have condemned the use of formaldehyde, but other preservatives, such as "lysol" (a cresylic compound) and "arasol," have no tanning effect and may be used with safety.

After the operation of fleshing, it is necessary to get rid of the lime in the hides, for, if they were put directly into tan liquors, the lime, being alkaline, would neutralise the acidity of the tan liquors and retard the beginning of the tanning process for a long period. The leather would ultimately be poor, thin, stained, and brittle.

Up to the process of deliming, there is not a great deal of difference in preparing the hides and skins for the large variety of leathers, but between the fleshing and the tanning processes the work varies considerably, and largely determines the character of the finished leather. When the hides or skins are in the limed state, they are gristly and firm in texture. A certain amount of this firmness is desirable in some leathers, such as sole and belting, and, therefore, it is deemed advisable to leave a small quantity of lime in the hides, although, to get them evenly coloured in tanning, it is essential that the lime should be completely removed from the surface of the hide. An old method, which is even in use to-day in some tanneries, is to wash the fleshed hides in a cubical or hexagonal drum for several hours in running water, which is conveyed through an iron pipe in the journal of the drum, and escapes through small holes in the drum. The effect of using a hard water for washing out the lime is shown in the interior of these washing drums, the sides of which become incrustated with a thick, hard deposit. The surface of this incrustation is irregular, and small projections are sometimes formed which mark the hides and reduce their value, as the impressions are not removed in later processes.

The modern method of deliming hides intended for sole leather is to use a weak solution of acid, or an acid salt. For this purpose, sulphuric and hydrochloric acids are by far the cheapest, but require handling with great care, as any excess used has a corrosive and destructive effect on the fibres, which results in weak leather. Mild organic acids are much safer, and those generally preferred are lactic, formic, and butyric, although boracic and acetic acids are favoured by some tanners. Butyrate of ammonia is used for the same purpose by a number of French tanners. The same acid bath can be used for a second lot of hides, but sufficient acid should be added to raise the acidity of the liquor to its former standard. It is inadvisable to use one bath more than four or five times. The salt formed during the process by the combination of the lime with the acid-calcium lactate, formate, butyrate, acetate, or borate, according to the acid used-must be washed from the hides, either in a pit or drum, before they are ready for the tan liquors.

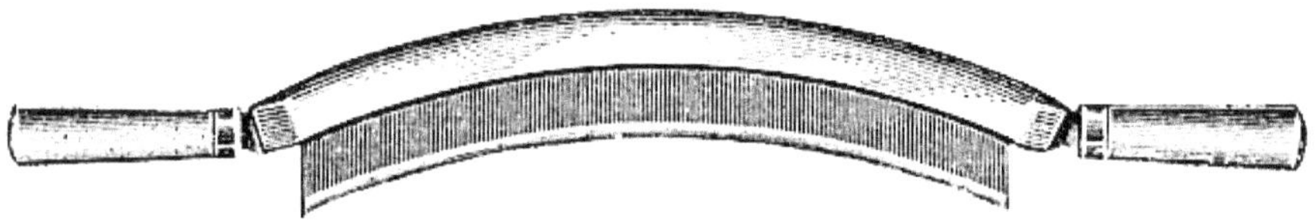

Fig. 20
SCUDDING KNIFE

Other kinds of hides and skins require additional treatment, according to the class of leather it is intended to make. Hides to be dressed for such purposes as bags, portmanteaus, cases, harness, belting, and stout uppers are usually steeped in an infusion of hen or pigeon dung. A vat is filled with tepid water, a quantity of the dung, usually about half a pailful, is added and well stirred in the water before putting the hides in. The acid fermentation evolved neutralises the lime, while bacteria multiply and rapidly reduce the rubbery limed hide to a soft, flaccid condition. The hides are then well washed in clear water and scudded, after which they are transferred to the tan pits. "Scudding" is the technical name of an operation performed on hides and skins with a special tool, known as the scudding knife, which consists of a convex piece of slate or vulcanite fitted into a wooden or steel handle (Fig. 20). The hides are placed on the beam, grain side up, and vigorously worked with the knife to scrape off scud (*i.e.*, short hairs, dirt, and soluble lime salts). Both sides of the hides should be scudded for best work. The process of treating hides with excrement is known technically as "bating,"

Calf skins, which are curried or dressed after tanning, should be reduced to a more supple condition than hides intended for harness, belting, and military leathers. A more active dung is, therefore, used for skins of all kinds which have to be rendered supple. Dog manure is generally used, that from the hunting kennels being preferred. Imported dry dung has to be used by some firms, as the supply of fresh dung is insufficient. The demand for the latter is very keen, as it is more effective than the dry product. Goat skins dressed for the famous shoe leather known as glazed or *glacé* kid, and kid skins for glove leather, need a larger proportion of "puer" than nearly every other kind of leather, for the grain of goat skins is naturally hard and requires a large quantity of dung to reduce it to the necessary softness and suppleness of "kid" leather.

Although these processes can only be described as disagreeable, they apparently have no injurious effect on the workmen. Further, the hides and skins are thoroughly cleaned before putting them in the tan liquors, in which the bacterial activity caused by the infusion of dung is quickly arrested.

Fortunately, from the hygienic point of view, the use of natural "bates" and "puers," although still extensive, is likely to be superseded everywhere by artificial products. So far there are nearly 2,000 tanneries throughout the world where the artificial bating materials are preferred, German and American tanners being the principal users.

The best known artificial bate is "Oropon," which consists of a mixture of pancreatin or trypsin, ammonium salts, and a large quantity of sawdust, the last-named merely acting as a mechanical agent. The enzyme, pancreatin, is the active ingredient, and may be prepared from the intestines of the pig. It has the effect of breaking up the albuminous matters of hides and skins, which are rapidly reduced to a soft and supple condition, while the ammonium salts cleanse them. The quantities used vary according to the degree of suppleness required in the finished leather.

The patentee and vendor of this proprietary article claims that it is suitable for all classes of leather. Hides for sole leather are sometimes treated with a weak "Oropon" liquor in Continental tanneries and, as a result of the cleansing properties of this bating material and its effect in opening up the fibres, the tannage proceeds rapidly. The use of enzymes for bating was discovered by an English leather manufacturer and chemist, who did not take out a patent for his invention, probably because he had previously patented and worked on a commercial scale a bacterial bate which gives very good results but requires much skill in application.

The artificial product, "Oropon," has many advantages over excrements. It is simpler, cleaner, and more rapid in working, and never damages the grain of the skin. On the contrary, great care and experience are needed in using excrements, and the skins may be so badly damaged through negligence as to be almost worthless. Bate burns are fairly frequent when dung is used, and are generally due to hard pieces being insufficiently broken up and diffused in the liquor.

Other useful artificial products are: "Erodin," and "Puerine," a patented American product which consists of a weak organic acid and a small proportion of molasses. Possibly, malt enzymes or diastase could be utilised for the manufacture of an artificial bate or puer, although they would not be so effective as animal products.

Where hides and skins have been treated with Oropon, they may be transferred to the tan liquors after being rinsed in water, although it is better to submit them to the operation of scudding.

There are two tests to determine the end of the process of bating and puering, although the extent to which the reduction is carried depends on the kind of leather wanted. For this reason, it is not advisable to remove every trace of lime from hides which must possess a certain degree of firmness when finished into leather. Of the two tests, one is chemical and the other mechanical. In the former case, a cross section is made in the thickest part of the hide and a few drops of phenolphthalein are added to the cross section; if the whole of the lime has been removed, no coloration is given, but, if lime be present, a purplish colour is given, which varies in intensity according to the contents of lime in the hide. The other test is made by pressure with the thumb nail, and, if the impression be permanent, the hides or skins are in a sufficiently reduced, or, as it is technically known, "fallen" condition for all practical purposes. The latter test is really only useful when the process has to be carried to its fullest practical extent, as it affords no idea of the intermediate stage. The experienced workman can judge the progress made by appearance and touch.

In cases where skins have been puered with excrement it is often necessary, after scudding them, to submit them to a further process before tanning. This is known as "drenching," and consists in treating the skins in an infusion of wheaten bran or pea flour. The acid fermentation produced by these ingredients effectually cleanses the skins by neutralising the last traces of lime and scud, and prepares them in an ideal condition for the process of tanning. The combined processes of bating with Oropon and drenching in bran are extremely useful for skins to be dressed into glove leather.

Following the processes of bating, puering, or drenching, the skins are washed in water to remove all mechanical impurities, and are then in a perfectly clean condition for tanning.

CHAPTER VI TANNING PROCESSES

The methods of tanning may be classified as follow: (1) Vegetable tanning processes; (2) methods of chroming; (3) tawing processes; (4) oil tannages; (5) formaldehyde tannages; (6) sundry tannages, chiefly mineral; and (7) combination tannages. The public is chiefly familiar with types of vegetable tannage in boot sole, bag, and portmanteau leathers; of chrome tannage, in box calf and glazed kid used for boot uppers; of the tawing process, in kid glove leather; and of the oil tannage in wash leather or "chamois."

VEGETABLE TANNING PROCESSES

The methods of tanning with infusions of barks, leaves, and fruits of trees and plants containing tannin are much more numerous than they were a decade ago, and tanners have now to pay special attention to the selection and blending of the materials they use in order to produce the various qualities of leather required. Formerly, most of the sole leather was tanned in oak bark liquors, and, in the later stages of the process, valonia and gambier were added to quicken the process and give solidity to the leather. This tannage, which may be described as an oak bark tannage, is still used by a few tanners, but the wide choice of materials available has brought other tanning agents into prominence, chiefly because they possess more astringent properties, and, therefore, tan more quickly than oak bark. Moreover, the need of other materials than oak bark became a necessity several years ago, as the supply of the latter would be inadequate to produce the large quantity of leather now required, even allowing for the rapid development of mineral tannages. Further, it is amply proved that a good blend of materials (mixed tannage) produces quite as durable and a firmer leather than the old oak bark tannage; unfortunately, there are other blends, occasionally combined with extraneous weighting materials, which account for the poor quality of a great deal of modern sole leather.

While the mixed tannage is now popular for sole, belting, harness, and other heavy leathers, vegetable tanned light skins, such as calf, goat, and sheep, are in most cases treated with a single material, sumach being used for a good proportion of them.

Whichever method be used, the first essential is the most suitable means of leaching the materials, or extracting the tannin. It seems, however, that this process may be eventually eliminated from the tannery, for most tanning materials are now converted into extracts, which only require dissolving in water to prepare the tan liquor. The manufacture of tanning extracts is quite a separate business, which is generally, but not always, conducted in factories situated near the source of the raw materials. There are important extract works in the Argentine, Paraguay, Canada, the United States, Hungary, North Germany, Borneo, Smyrna, France, Italy, and England.

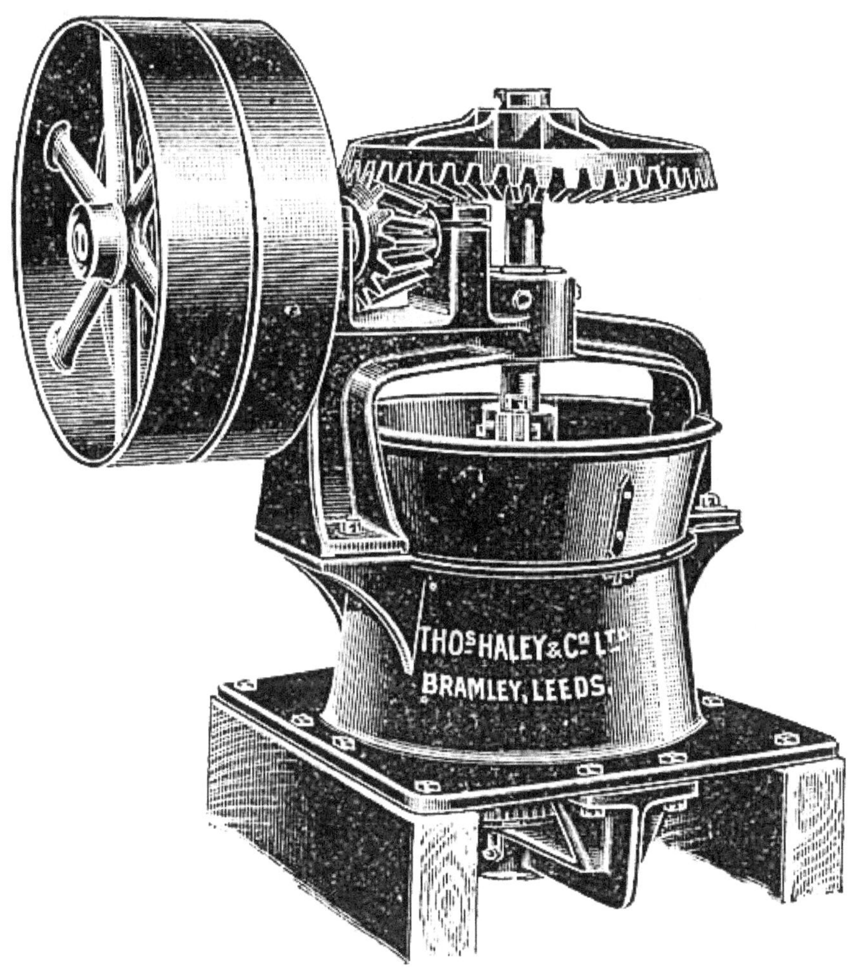

Fig. 21

BARK MILL

Where natural tanning materials are used, either entirely or in conjunction with extracts, the leaching is done in a series of large square pits, four of which would suffice for a small yard, while a very large tanning would need twelve or sixteen. Oak bark, which is usually delivered to the tannery in strips measuring 3 to 6 ft. in length, must be chopped or ground into small pieces by machine (Fig. 21 bark_mill). A measured quantity (a certain number of baskets or skeps full) is placed in the empty pits, which are then filled with water. The liquor is pumped from these pits, as required, to others in which the hides are tanned. The hard fruit of myrobalans, which somewhat resembles nutmegs, is powdered in a disintegrator or special crusher.

FIG. 22
TAN-YARD
("Dri-ped" Tannery)

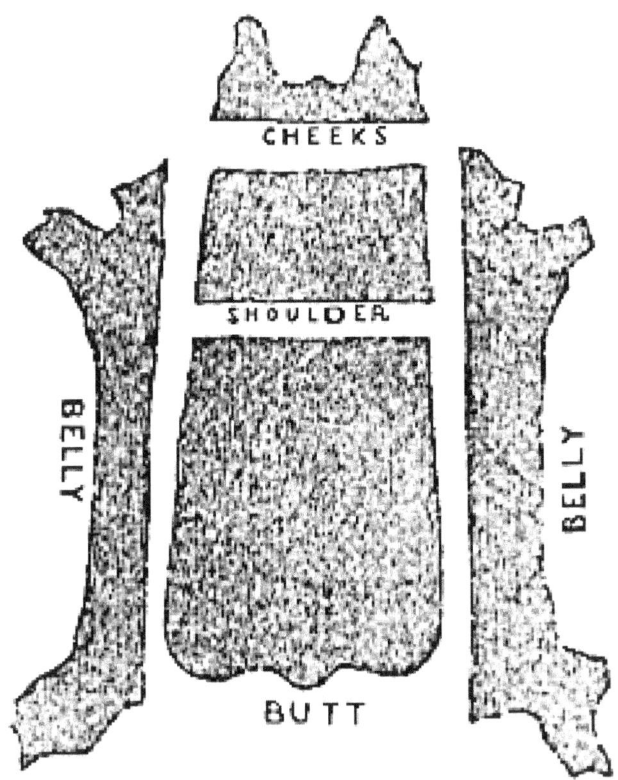

FIG. 23
HIDE ROUNDED FOR SOLE
LEATHER

The three principal vegetable tannages are those for sole, dressing, and light leathers, and it is obvious that a careful selection of materials is necessary to obtain the desired effects. For this reason, oak bark, although a good tanning material for dressing leather, is insufficient to produce a firm sole leather, and, therefore, even in the so-called pure bark tannages, valonia or other suitable tannin is used towards the end of the process in order to increase the solidity and waterproof quality of the leather. There are two general methods of tanning sole leather, namely, the pit and the drum tannage. In the first case, the hides are passed through three series of pits containing gradually increased strengths of tannin (Fig. 22). These series are technically described as "suspenders" or "colouring pits," "handlers," and "layers" or "layaways." To facilitate handling and economise tanning materials, hides are "rounded" (i.e., cut into sections) either before tanning or after the hides have passed through the suspenders (Fig. 23). The obvious advantage of the former method is that the offal (shoulders and bellies) removed can be chrome tanned if required. The suspenders may consist of any number of pits from six to twenty-four, according to the size of the tannery. As the name implies, the hides are suspended in the liquors from poles, which extend across the top of the pit. The hides are attached to the poles by means of stout cord or copper hooks. Various mechanical appliances are in use to supersede the old method of allowing the hides to rest during this process. These methods save time and tend to produce even coloration, the latter being a very important point in the early stages of tanning. Some of the methods advocated, however, are too vigorous for the hides at this stage, when the chief object should be to preserve as much gelatine as possible. The best mechanical system is that which gently raises and lowers the hides in the liquors. Some of the American tanners use a mechanical contrivance known as the rocker, which consists of a stout wooden beam rocking from a central pivot, and with a see-saw movement. The objection to this method is that the hides do not receive equal treatment, those in the centre receiving hardly any movement, while others at the ends of the beam are raised too far out of the liquor. Under these conditions, the colouring of the leather must be irregular. Another method, invented in England, consists in suspending the hides from a wooden frame which can be mechanically moved on wheels.

As the contact of tanning liquors with iron must be avoided to prevent discoloration (iron and tannin form the basis of inks), the wheels should be galvanized. This mechanical method is very satisfactory, for the hides are moved gently and kept in the liquors. As some tannins oxidise rapidly (*i.e.*, darken in colour by exposure to the air), any process which exposes the hides at this stage for lengthy periods should be avoided.

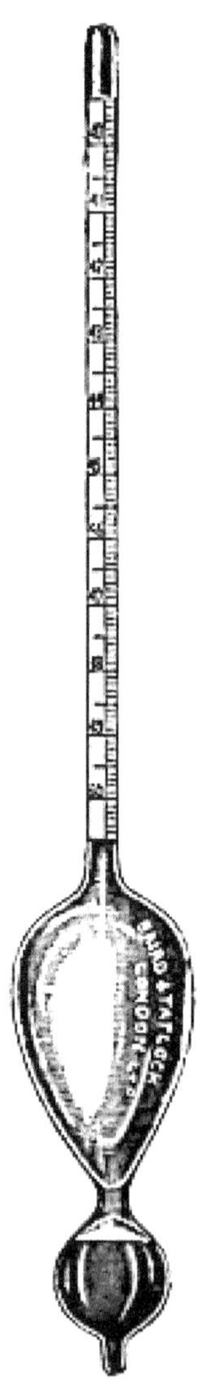

FIG. 24
BARKOMETER

The theory of the vegetable tanning process is not perfectly understood, and the principal trade chemists are not yet agreed as to whether the changes are chemical, physical, or both. Many are inclined to believe that both changes take place, and this view is probably correct, as a pure tannic acid produces a thin, empty leather, while a tanning material which contains a fair proportion of non-tannin matters, yields a full and firm leather. The practical tanner who adapts his work to the theory that tanning is a process of feeding the hides with gradually increasing strengths of tannin, is, in any event, on the right track. The suspender liquors are always weak in tannin, and are pumped from "handler" liquors through which packs of hides have already passed. It is important that these liquors possess a certain degree of acidity, and, if the natural acids of the tan liquor are too weak, or neutralised completely by the lime in a pack of hides that has been treated, a small quantity of acetic, formic, or lactic acid is added. Formic acid has the additional advantage of making the liquor antiseptic. It is absolutely necessary that the liquors have acid properties, otherwise tanning cannot proceed. Acid assists penetration of tannin. Hyposulphite of soda, formaldehyde, or synthetic tannin may be used for the same purpose, while these also help to keep the leather light in colour, owing to their bleaching properties. After passing through three or four suspender pits, in which the tan liquor is gradually strengthened, the hides are often rounded and the butts (Fig. 23) are transferred to the handlers. The first handler liquor should register about 25 degrees by the barkometer (Fig. 24), an instrument which registers the density of tan liquors. The handlers consist of a series of six or eight, and the strength of the liquors should be increased gradually. After a day's immersion in the first handler liquor, the hides are hauled out with a sharp two-pronged hook fixed to the end of a long wooden pole, similar to that used in the liming process. After they have been piled up for a few hours, two workmen, one on each side of the pit, place the hides flat in the next pit. The tan liquor is then run off the first handler to the suspender and fresh liquor is pumped into the empty pit, which then becomes the head or strongest liquor of the series. The succeeding packs will, therefore, follow in rotation: the first going to No. 2 pit, the second to No. 3, and so on. In the last two or three handler pits, the hides are sometimes dusted with freshly ground tanning material, such as oak bark, myrobalans, or divi-divi, the object being to strengthen the tan liquor so that it penetrates the hides before they are transferred to the layers. The handler liquors, which are originally sent back from the layers, are also frequently strengthened by the addition of oakwood, chestnut, or quebracho extracts, although some tanners only use extracts in the layers. Gambier is a useful material at this stage, as it keeps the liquors mellow and plumps the leather. In the layers, the last series of tan pits, the hides are treated with very strong extracts, and are also heavily dusted with such natural tanning materials as give firmness and solidity to the leather. For this purpose, nothing is better than valonia, or valonia extract, which deposits a large quantity of bloom, or ellagic acid. Where a mixed tannage of natural materials is used, the density of the liquors may reach 50 degrees barkometer, but if strong extracts be added, the barkometer may exceed 100 degrees. The relation between the layers and handlers in regard to the disposal of the used liquors is similar to that between handlers and suspenders; the first layer used is sent to the last handler.

By the English method, the leather is not, as a rule, transferred immediately from one pit to another, as it is found preferable to lay the hides in pile for a few hours, by which means the great weight helps to force the tannin through them. By draining the hides, they are in good condition for the absorption of the next tan liquor. The English method of handling is too slow for most of the American tanneries, where the greater proportion of the hides are cut straight down the centre to form "sides," as they are technically known. In America, the pieces of leather, whether hides, butts, bellies, or shoulders, are often tied together and transferred from one pit to another by means of a skeleton reel, worked either by hand or mechanically. The latest type of reel is a great improvement on the old reel. The cost of manual labour in many English tanneries is very great, in view of the fact that the hides have to pass through many pits, and the work of transferring the hides from one pit to another is done entirely by hand. It seems that there is plenty of scope for mechanical ingenuity in overcoming this difficulty, and it may yet be found possible to construct a perforated brass platform, connected with a crane, by which the whole of the hides could be lifted out in a second, left to drain for half an hour or more, and then bodily transferred to, and lowered in, the next pit. Naturally, it is easier, and quite within the bounds of practicability, to raise the hides from suspenders by mechanical power, as it would not be difficult to fix a stout cross-beam to the pulley from which the hides are suspended. The leather can be safely treated with very astringent tannin in the last series of pits, and the use of strong extracts is, therefore, a common practice at that stage, not only to give solidity and firmness to the leather, but to increase its weight.

It would be quite fatal to the production of good leather if strong tannins were used in the early stages of the process, because the surface on both sides would tan quickly, the grain of the hide would be badly drawn owing to the sensitiveness of gelatine to astringent solutions, and it would be impossible to make the tannin penetrate the hide. The final product would be a half-tanned leather which would be extremely brittle and poor in quality; in fact, quite unsuitable for sole leather. Despite the well-known axiom that the vegetable tannage (but not the mineral) must proceed slowly and gradually in the early stages of the process if the hides are to be properly tanned, the modern tendency is to speed up the tanning, with the result that, in some cases, the so-called sole leather is really not fit for the purpose for which it is intended. The root of the evil is the desperate attempt made by many boot manufacturers to produce lower-priced boots than those of their competitors.

Taking into account the development of leather trades chemistry, it is not surprising that the problem of reducing the time required to complete the old processes of tanning has received much attention. The results have been successful in some instances and have certainly proved that very good sole leather can be made without leaving the hides in the pits for a year or longer.

It has also been shown that the absorption of tannin can be accelerated by treating the hides, before putting them in the suspenders, with a solution of acid (lactic or butyric for preference), or hyposulphite of soda, or synthetic tannin. The latter penetrates the hides in a few hours without contracting the grain, increases the solubility of the vegetable tannins subsequently used, and helps to keep the leather light and uniform in colour. It is of no use alone for heavy leathers, however, as it lacks the physical properties necessary to make the leather firm and resistant to water. The use of "soluble" oils in the tan liquors is another late innovation which has given good results. The term "soluble" in connection with oils merely means that they are made miscible with water by treating them with acids. Solubilised cod oil might be specially useful, as it has tanning properties and would increase the wearing and waterproof qualities of the leather. The chief objects of using oil in tanning, however, are to increase the weight of the leather and permit the use of strong liquors.

The tanning process outlined is the oak bark tannage, which is now supplanted in many yards by the mixed tannage, in which various tannins, chiefly exotic, are skilfully blended to produce the kind of leather wanted. Each tannin seems to have special characteristics, although the materials are classified into only three groups, namely: pyrogallol, catechol, and mixed (pyrogallol and catechol) tannins. Generally, the best mixed tannages for solid leather consist of a combination of both pyrogallol and catechol tannins. Reviewing the characteristics of some of the principal tanning materials, it may be said that oak bark produces a nice, fawn-coloured leather of strong texture, but tans slowly; valonia makes the leather solid, durable, and waterproof; myrobalans quicken the process and lighten the objectionable colour of other tannins; divi-divi and algarobilla are very rich in tannin, and are, therefore, useful in later stages of the process; gambier mellows the astringency of other liquors and plumps the leather; while most of the tanning extracts on the market penetrate the hides much more quickly, often give a lighter colour than that produced by solutions of the natural materials, and expedite the process considerably.

The most popular tanning materials are: oakwood, quebracho, chestnut, valonia, myrobalan, mangrove, mimosa, hemlock and spruce extracts, oak bark, valonia, gambier and sumach. The following are some of the combinations in use —

For Sole Leather.

1. Oak bark and valonia, or valonia extract.
  2. Oak bark, valonia, and gambier.
  3. Oak bark, quebracho extract, and myrobalan extract.
  4. Chestnut, quebracho and valonia extracts.
  5. Chestnut and oakwood extracts.
  6. Oakwood and quebracho extracts, and divi-divi or algarobilla.
  7. Quebracho extract, myrobalans, and valonia.
  8. Quebracho, mangrove, and valonia extracts.
  9. Oakwood, mimosa, and valonia extracts.
  10. Hemlock and oak extracts (American union tannage).

For Dressing Leathers.

1. Oak bark and sumach.
    2. Oakwood and quebracho extracts, and sumach.
    3. Synthetic tannin and oakwood extract.
    4. Synthetic tannin and myrobalans.
    5. Gambier and sumach.
    6. Wattle bark and myrobalans.

Sumach is often used alone for some classes of goat, sheep, and calf skins. Synthetic tannins can also be used alone for light leathers.

Many other variations may be tabulated, for nearly every tanner has his own recipe, having found by experience the blend of tannage that best suits his trade.

Apart from these innumerable combinations, the only method whereby the vegetable tanning process may be hastened is the mechanical, for which purpose either the paddle (Fig. 25) or the drum (Fig. 13) is used. The former consists of a wheel constructed of wooden shelves which, when in motion, dip a little way into the tan liquor in a vat, and so keep it in constant circulation. The drum is fitted inside with wooden shelves or pegs, which carry some of the hides or skins to the top of the drum at each revolution. Were it not for these shelves, the tannage would probably be irregular or otherwise unsatisfactory, as the hides would always be heaped together at the bottom of the drum. The paddles and drum are more often used for light than for heavy leather, as they not only have the effect of making the leather loose on the grain, but also make it soft and supple, characteristics which are not required in most of the heavy leathers.

Fig. 25

PADDLE VAT

However, the drum is now largely used on the Continent for the tannage of sole leather. A great saving in the cost of production is thereby effected, but the leather, although of satisfactory appearance, lacks the durability and waterproof quality of pit-tanned leather. The process is much simpler than the pit method, and less room is required. There are only two stages of tanning: (1) by placing the hides in colouring pits or suspenders, in which the hides are nearly struck through with tannin; and (2) running them in slowly-revolving drums containing solutions of tannin which are gradually strengthened until the process is finished. There can be no doubt that the tannin is rapidly forced between the fibres of the hide by mechanical action, but it is not so firmly combined as that slowly absorbed by the hide in the pit method. This can be proved by placing two pieces of weighed leather-one tanned in pits and the other in a drum-for twenty-four hours, drying the leather and reweighing it, when it will be found that the drum-tanned leather has lost the greater percentage of weight. To obviate this disadvantage as far as possible, use is made of special oils, which serve to fix the tannin more firmly between the fibres and render the leather more resistant to water. Other frequent drawbacks of drum tanning are looseness of grain and lack of substance. In sole leather tanning, the former is modified to some extent by extra pressure in rolling the leather during the finishing operations; while the latter difficulty is sometimes overcome by swelling the leather with acid and then fixing the swollen condition of the hide by treating it with a weak solution of formaldehyde. This chemical also has tanning properties, so that the process is hastened; but leather prepared in this way cannot be as durable as that produced by a natural tannage.

It seems that the aid of the engineer is necessary to overcome the difficulty of looseness of the grain caused by the severe pounding of the hides in the drums. The constant circulation of the tan liquor is required, but the hides should only be subjected to gentle motion. It is true there are tanning drums on the market which are said to obviate all the difficulty found in making sole leather in ordinary drums fitted with shelves or pegs, but a drum that meets the ideal conditions for the production of a solid yet flexible sole leather has not yet been invented. It seems that a kind of inner framework, to which the hides can be attached and which rotates much more slowly than the main drum, may solve the problem. The drum tannage permits the use of an excessive quantity of tannin, which, of course, adds to the weight of the leather. By the drum method of tanning, heavy hides can be tanned in two days after leaving the colouring pits; lighter hides are, naturally, tanned in less time, proportionate to their substance. The pit method occupies any time from one to fifteen months, although nowadays very few hides are left in the tan pits for a year.

The methods of tanning just described relate chiefly to sole leather, but there is an enormous production of leather known as dressing hides, which are tanned, dried in the rough state, and sent to curriers or leather dressers for finishing. These hides are used for numerous purposes, including bags, portmanteaus, harness, saddlery, straps, belting, and boot uppers. The tannage of dressing hides differs slightly from that of sole leather; the liquors must be mellower and contain less insoluble matter, in order to obtain the necessary pliability, and a good, clear colour on the grain. A satisfactory tannage is obtained by treating the hides in oak bark liquors, which, in the later stages of the process, may be strengthened with oak wood, or myrobalan extract, or pure gambier, and completing the process in a tepid bath of sumach, which clears and lightens the colour. The drum is more suitable for the tannage of dressing hides than it is for sole leather. A quick method of drum tanning would be to treat the hides first in a 5 per cent. solution of neradol, the artificial tannin, and then complete the process with oakwood, chestnut, or quebracho extracts, or even in mixtures of these extracts. In this way, fairly good leather could be made in about two days. Neradol prevents the drawn grain and dark coloration that would result from the use of vegetable extracts alone.

In the case of light skins, such as calf, goat, and sheep, the method of vegetable tannage again differs from those just described, although there is a fair quantity of calf skins tanned with oak bark, especially those used in the shoe trade. The tendency, however, is to complete the process rapidly by using extracts, such as oakwood, quebracho, or mimosa. A very good tannage for the production of a mellow and plump leather is that of pure gambier, the colour produced forming a good ground for brown shades. Where light, fancy colours are required on the finished leather, this tannage must be completed by placing the skins in a tepid bath of sumach.

A large proportion of the vegetable-tanned sheep and goat skins is produced by sumach alone, which was adjudged by the Commission appointed a few years ago by the Royal Society of Arts to investigate the cause of decay in bookbinding leather to be the best tanning material and the one least affected by exterior conditions, such as gas, sunlight, air and dust.

Many sheep skins are split into two sections by machine before tanning, the top portion, known as the grain, being tanned in sumach, and described as "skivers." The under section, the side near the carcase, is known in the trade as a "lining," and is usually made into the so-called "chamois" leather by means of the oxidation of fish oils.

Other noteworthy vegetable tannages are those used in the production of Russia leather, and a large proportion of East India leather. Real Russia leather, of which the raw material consists of small native hides and calf skins, has a characteristic and pleasant odour, which is derived from the birch and willow barks used in the tanning process. Birch bark contains an essential oil, which is permanently fixed on the fibres of the leather during the process of tanning. This leather is only produced in Russia, and chiefly in one large tannery, although imitations are made in Great Britain, America, and Germany. These are produced by the use of ordinary tanning materials, and the scent is applied, either during or after the dyeing process by the addition of birch tar oil, which is made by the distillation of birch bark. In some respects, for example, in brilliance of finish, smoothness of grain, and freedom from defects, the imitation is better than the real, but the latter has the great advantage that its perfume is of superior fragrance and permanent, whereas the imitation leather only retains the odour for about a year. It is somewhat remarkable, in view of the good demand that exists for the leather, especially in England and Germany, that no firm outside Russia has thought it worth while to produce the genuine article. The tannage would be particularly serviceable for bookbinding leather, as the oil of the birch has both insecticidal and antiseptic properties.

The principal vegetable tannage used for Indian leather, namely, the bark of the *acacia arabica*, known to the natives as babul, or babool, has quite a contrary effect, for it contains a large quantity of red colouring matter, which is incorporated with the leather in the tanning process, and although it shows very little in the rough-tanned leather, it is apt to darken if the finished leather is exposed to strong light for a long period. This oxidation is accompanied by a gradual weakening of the fibres of the leather, which is, therefore, quite unsuitable for bookbinding. Fortunately, Indian tanners are making rapid progress in using other tanning materials, a good number of which are found in India.

Although the bark of the *acacia arabica* is not altogether satisfactory, the pods of the same tree, which are commercially known as "bablah" and contain nearly twice as much tannin as the bark, produce a very light-coloured, almost white, leather, and it is asserted that this material is a valuable substitute for sumach.

Mineral Tannages

By far the most important of the mineral tannages is the chrome process, the merits and demerits of which have not only been freely discussed in the trade, but also in the lay press. Fanciful theories of the poisonous character of this kind of leather have been published from time to time in the daily press. Such absurd statements as that prussic acid and mercury are used in the manufacture of chrome leather hardly need refuting, as, even if they could convert skins into leather, the cost would prohibit their use. The only poisonous acid used in one of the many chrome processes is chromic acid, but this is converted into the oxide of chromium in a second bath and is, therefore, made quite innocuous.

The chrome tannage is effected either by the one-bath method or the two-bath. In the former case, the tanning agent, either a basic chromium sulphate or chloride, is present in the one liquor used; in the latter method, the hides or skins are impregnated with a solution of chromic acid, which is reduced to chromic oxide in a second bath consisting of sulphurous acid and a small quantity of free sulphur. The properties of leather produced by the two-bath process render it especially suitable for vulcanising on rubber; hence its large use for non-skidding bands for motor tyres.

There are several recipes for making one-bath liquors. A favourite mixture consists of chrome alum and sodium carbonate (common soda). Another method consists of reducing a solution of chromic acid with glucose or grape-sugar. This liquor has a greater plumping effect on the leather than the chrome alum liquor has. A third process of making a one-bath liquor combines the use of bichromate of potash and chrome alum, which, when dissolved, is converted into a basic chrome salt by means of a reducing agent. The one-bath liquor can be easily and safely applied to hides and skins, and is used in much the same manner as a vegetable tan liquor, beginning with a weak solution and gradually increasing the strength until the process is completed. The two-bath method needs great care, as a slight difference in the proportions of the ingredients used may alter the character of the leather produced.

The formula now largely used is practically the same as that of the original patentee, Augustus Schultz, an American chemist. The first bath, the chromic acid solution, is made by treating bichromate of potash or soda with hydrochloric, sulphuric, or formic acids. Bichromate of potash and hydrochloric acid (commonly known as muriatic acid, or spirits of salts) are commonly used, and in the proportion of 5 per cent. and 2-1/2 per cent. of the weight of the drained pelts (5 lb. of bichromate and 2-1/2 lb. of acid for 100 lb. of pelts). The chemical reaction is represented by the following equation—

$$K_2Cr_2O_7 + 2HCl = 2KCl + 2CrO_3 + H_2O$$

Bichromate of potash + Hydrochloric Acid = Potassium chloride + chromic acid + water.

This process is most conveniently carried out in the paddle-vat (Fig. 25), which, in this case, should be fitted with a wooden cover to exclude light, since the colour of the chromic acid liquor is affected by strong light. Some chrome tanners prefer to use the drum tumbler (Fig. 13), but the pounding of the skins by this method is apt to make the grain loose. Whichever method be adopted, the hides or skins should be horsed up to drain for several hours before transferring them to the second bath. It is important that they be placed grain to grain and smoothed out, as creases and air bubbles between the skins become fixed in the second liquor, and depreciate the value of the finished leather. To avoid this danger, many tanners pass the hides or skins through a striking-out machine under light pressure. Another detail of importance is to cover the chromed skins with canvas or matting to keep them from the light. Although the skins are preserved by chromic acid, they are not made into leather, for in this condition they would dry quite horny. Hence, it is undesirable that the hides should be dried at this stage and sold as leather, although such a proceeding has been attempted. Further, chromic acid is an irritant poison which may cause an eruption on the hands and arms of workers handling the hides in this solution, unless they are protected by rubber gloves, or by coating the hands with a mixture of vaseline and lanoline. The second bath consists of chemicals which reduce the chromic acid to the oxide, which is quite inert, so that there is no danger whatever of contracting a poisoned foot as the result of wearing chrome leather. The chemicals largely used for the second bath are hyposulphite of soda and hydrochloric acid. Sodium sulphite may also be used without the addition of acid. The skins change from an orange colour to a pale, bluish-grey tint, but the process is not completed until a cross section shows that the colour has changed right through the skin. A suitable proportion is 10 per cent. "hypo" and 2-1/2 per cent. acid (28° Twaddell) calculated on the weight of the drained pelts. Calf, goat, and sheep skins are usually treated in the drum, but hides, especially if a certain degree of firmness is required, are preferably run in the paddle-vat. The reaction of the chemicals in the second bath are somewhat complicated, but the principal point is the reduction of the chromic acid (CrO_3) to chromic oxide (Cr_{23}).

The sulphurous acid produced acts as the reducing agent, but is not freely liberated until towards the end of the process, the skins first changing into a dirty brown colour which gradually gives place to a beautiful pale-bluish tint. The last stages of the process are also marked by the formation of free sulphur, which aids materially in softening the leather, and giving the two-bath chrome tanned leather its characteristic rubbery texture. The vats in which this process is carried out should always be fitted with lids to confine the strong sulphurous fumes. By adding an excess of "hypo," the skins can be bleached until they are nearly white. This has no harmful effect on the leather, but makes it softer, though somewhat looser on the grain. When completely tanned, the skins are horsed up again, left to drain for at least twenty-four hours, and are then ready for dressing and finishing.

The recipes for the one-bath process are numerous, but it is becoming a common practice for tanners to buy the liquors or extracts already prepared in chemical works, which are, naturally, better fitted up for the production of a more uniform material than it would be possible to make in most tanneries.

Combination Tannages

Combination tannages have steadily grown in favour during the last few years, and will probably have an important bearing on future methods of tanning. Among those found practicable are: (1) Vegetable and chrome; (2) vegetable and alum; (3) alum and chrome; (4) synthetic and natural tannins; (5) synthetic and chrome; (6) alum and synthetic; (7) formaldehyde and chrome; (8) chrome and iron.

CHAPTER VII THE DRESSING, DYEING, AND FINISHING OF LEATHER

The dressing and finishing of leathers of all kinds seems to be of growing importance every year, despite the fact that the durability of leather is often impaired by the chemicals and heavy machinery used in order to get a clear and bright colour or a highly-glazed finish. One exception to this rule, however, is japanned and enamelled leathers made by the new collodion-amyl acetate process, which not only produces the so-called "patent" finish, but also adds to the strength of the leather.

Dressing and finishing may be conveniently classified in four sections —

1. Finishing of boot sole leather.

2. Dyeing and finishing of machine belting, strap, harness, and other heavy greasy leathers.

3. Dyeing and finishing of boot, portmanteau, case, bookbinding, hat, and upholstery leathers, and of the numerous fancy leathers.

4. Dressing, dyeing, and finishing of glove and chamois leathers.

There are also a few special kinds of leather which do not come within the scope of this list. The limited size of this book makes it impossible to outline the finishing of all kinds of leather, and only a few of the important varieties can be referred to in the following pages.

Sole Leather

Formerly, the finishing of sole leather was a fairly easy matter, as the slow process of tanning with oak bark which was in general use gave the latter a nice fawn colour. The modern tendency, however, is to demand even lighter-coloured leather than that produced by an oak bark tannage, and, as most of the mixed tannages impart a darker colour, the practice of bleaching has been universally adopted. This process is to be greatly deprecated, since it reduces the strength of the leather. Further, it has the serious drawback of removing matters which would add to the waterproof quality of the leather, and yet the boot manufacturers demand light-coloured sole leather. As in many other articles of modern manufacture, quality is sacrificed for appearance. The colour of sole leather is of no importance whatever to the wearer of the boot, and the public should make a strong protest against bleached sole leather, and also against leather weighted with adulterants, if they wish to get boots of good wearing quality. It is difficult to know where the finishing of some of the modern sole leather begins. Formerly, the line of demarcation between tanning and finishing was distinct, for the finishing processes were begun as soon as the hides were sufficiently tanned. This is by no means the case to-day, as, in many cases, the finishing may be said to begin with a supplementary but unnecessary tannage in very strong tanning extracts, with the object of making the leather firm and plump, and, incidentally, imparting additional weight. This practice would be discontinued if sole leather were sold by superficial measurement. On the other hand, those who favour the continuance of the present system of selling by weight assert that the adoption of the measurement system would indubitably result in the production of a lot of under-tanned leather, that mechanical means would be devised to stretch the leather and thus give it an artificial area, and that a fair quantity of the leather produced does not lie flat, and would, therefore, be difficult to measure correctly. A great point in favour of selling by measurement is that there would be no necessity to weight the leather, and a mere visual examination would suffice to determine the quality, whereas it is often difficult to state whether leather has been treated with injurious artificial matters or not, and certainly impossible to determine the extent of this fraud, without a careful and somewhat elaborate analysis. Of course, there are some rough practical tests for ascertaining the quality of sole leather, especially in regard to the extent of its resistance to water. A weighed quantity of the leather is soaked in water for twenty-four hours, taken out, squeezed, dried, and reweighed. If the loss of weight does not exceed 5 per cent., the leather is a good sample and well tanned; on the other hand, it does not follow that a loss, say, of 40 per cent., would indicate adulteration with injurious materials, as the leather may have been tanned with an excess of strong extracts which have not properly combined with the fibres, with the result that the excess is easily removed in contact with water. However, methods of fixing tanning extracts on the fibres of the leather have been devised (see p. 117). A careful note should be made of the time required to soak the leather through; if water is absorbed rapidly, the leather is, naturally, unfit for soles.

After the tanner has taken great pains to produce the paleness of tint required, the shoemaker buffs away the grain, thereby reducing the resistance of the leather to wear, and then generally covers it with a black, tan, or white dressing. In its turn, this finish is likewise spoiled the first time the leather is worn. There could be nothing more futile than the elaborate finishing of sole leather to make it pale in colour, as it means that fully 80 per cent. of the leather produced has to be bleached in some way or other; and the manner in which this process is effected has a direct influence on reducing the wearing quality of the leather. If, for example, the colour of the leather is brightened with myrobalans, or sumach, or with extracts of these materials, the wearing quality is not affected; unfortunately, this method is not largely used, as it does not increase the weight of the leather and would tend to make it soft. A large proportion of sole leather is treated with strong sulphited extracts, which both bleach and increase the weight of the leather. In some cases, the leather is placed in vats containing hot tanning extracts to increase the bleaching effect and add to the weight. The gain of weight by this surplus tannage may be, and often is, from 8 per cent. to 10 per cent., and, whereas the tanner a century ago used to get only slightly above 50 per cent. of leather on the weight of the raw hide, it is no uncommon thing nowadays to get a yield of nearly 70 per cent.

The tanners are hardly to be blamed for this practice, which really ought to be stopped; it is almost entirely due to the demand of buyers for leather at a low price per lb., irrespective of its superficial area compared with a higher-priced and often cheaper article. It is only fair to state that those boot manufacturers who have taken careful costings of their leather have not suffered great loss in this way, but most repairers buy common leather in order to be able to do their work at fixed prices usual in this trade. A large proportion of this leather is under-tanned or weighted, and, in either case, absorbs water like a sponge. This kind of leather is quite unfit for soles, and ought to be condemned, as it not only absorbs moisture but also retains it for a long time, so that it is frequently a cause of colds and other complaints arising from chills.

If the repairer does not cost his leather as accurately as the wholesale boot manufacturer, the latter often neglects to take into account the quality of the leather, so long as cheap soles can be cut from it.

The continual demand for leather which will yield low-priced soles has brought about another practice which is much worse than the use of hot extracts. In this case, the hides are not tanned thoroughly, but, instead of completing the process with tanning extracts, the leather is treated with cheap chemicals, such as epsom salts (magnesium sulphate), glucose, and barium salts. These add considerable weight and save the cost of expensive tanning materials; further, it is claimed that they give increased firmness and substance to the thinner parts of the leather, which otherwise could not be used for soles. It is conceivable, therefore, that leather of this kind could be cut to greater advantage than that properly tanned, but, since this artificial filling is washed out on the first contact with water and the leather rapidly deteriorates through attracting and retaining moisture, the fraud of the system is at once apparent.

Although the use of leather artificially weighted with hygroscopic chemicals is extremely detrimental to health, it was only during last year that laws were passed forbidding the adulteration of leather, and even these are inadequate. Strange to relate, the two countries where these legal measures have been taken, Australia and South Africa, enjoy for the most part a hot and dry climate, while it is in wet weather that adulterated leather is most harmful. However, to Australia belongs the honour of initiating legal measures against frauds in leather manufacture, and their praiseworthy action must soon be copied by other civilised countries.

On the other hand, it would be inadvisable to prohibit the addition of every other material except those with tanning properties. There are undoubtedly a few substances which, used in combination with the tanning materials, add to the strength and value of the leather, and it is the opinion of some tanners that great developments will take place in this direction. Certain oils, sulphonated in order to render them easily miscible with water, and known commercially as "soluble" oils, exercise a beneficial effect when mixed with the tan liquors, for they lubricate the fibres of the leather, assist penetration of and fix the tannin. The time required for the process is, therefore, much reduced, as strong liquors may be used without harmful effect. The oil also serves as a lubricant for the fibres, obviates the harshness and brittleness usually associated with rapidly-tanned leather, and fixed to the extent of about 3 per cent., must increase its durability. Best of all, from the tanner's point of view, there is a moderate increase of weight. There are two or three special tanning oils on the market.

A vegetable gummy product has lately been introduced to the trade which has been found to give remarkable results when used in conjunction with tanning materials. This gummy matter is extracted from vegetable seeds and is placed on the market under the name of Tragasol. Its composition is somewhat similar to that of tannins, the Tragasol Co.'s analysis showing it to contain 43.51 per cent. of carbon, 6.23 per cent. of hydrogen, 48.38 per cent. of oxygen, 0.39 per cent. of nitrogen, and 1.49 per cent. of ash. It is very largely used for strengthening and sizing textile fabrics, and seems destined to play an important part in the leather trade, for it has tanning properties, increases the strength of the leather, and considerably hastens the process.

Its most important advantage is that it permits successful tannage in the drum, thus effecting a great saving of time and labour.

Hitherto, rapid tannages have not been very successful, as they generally made the leather harsh and brittle, and lessened its durability. Leather tanned by previous rapid methods was also less waterproof than that tanned in pits by slow methods. All these defects are avoided by using Tragasol, which, when combined with tanning extracts, forms a curdy precipitate, described by the makers of Tragasol as cutiloid (contraction of cutis and colloid, cutis meaning "skin," and the Tragasol being, chemically, a colloid). The cutiloid tannage increases the water-resistant properties of leather, and prevents the oxidation and consequent darkening of the colour of the tanning material used with it. Tests have been made which show that cutiloid-tanned leather will withstand a fall of water 12 in. high for six weeks before complete penetration takes place; ordinary tannages do not often resist water for more than a few hours.

For the tannage of sole leather in the drum by the cutiloid process, about 120 per cent. of Tragasol and 40 per cent. of chestnut or oakwood extract are required; this quantity is divided into four equal portions, which are added to the drum successively at intervals of one hour. The hides should then be nearly tanned through, and the process is completed with strong extract (chestnut and quebracho, or myrobalans, according to the kind of leather required). After drumming the hides for ten hours, they should remain at rest for two hours, then drummed another hour, and so on, alternately, until the completion of the process, which may require from twenty-four to thirty-six hours, according to the substance of the hides. By this process, the yield of leather may exceed 60 per cent. of the weight of the raw pelts. This percentage of yield may be raised to 70 per cent. or more in the case of sole leather by steeping the hides in hot extract.

The action of acids in swelling gelatine is sometimes abused, particularly on the Continent and in America. As pointed out before, tan liquors must be mildly acid in character before the process can proceed, and, if the organic acids of the tanning materials are insufficient, the addition of a small quantity of formic, or lactic, or acetic acid is necessary; but, in many of the American acid tannages, an excessive quantity of mineral acid is used, with the object of swelling the hides. When in this condition, they rapidly absorb an abnormal quantity of tannin, and the finished leather is unnaturally thick. To make matters worse, the tannage is sometimes not completed, but, instead, the hides are treated ("doped") with hygroscopic chemicals, which not only increase the weight of the leather but also endanger the health of those who have to wear it. Most of the American tanneries make no secret of their use of these unnecessary chemicals, but assert that they are obliged to use them in order to meet competition, and because a large number of bootmakers insist on buying sole leather at a low price per lb. The Leather and Paper Department of the U.S.A. Bureau of Industry analysed several American leathers in 1913 and found that a large majority were artificially weighted with glucose and Epsom salts (magnesium sulphate). Barium compounds are also used for the same purpose, but the American tannages are apparently free of this adulterant. The results were published in a pamphlet by the United States Government, together with a list of the firms whose leathers were tested.

While the European tanners do not weight their leather so freely as the Americans with these chemicals, the practice of swelling the hides unduly is not unknown, with the difference that, especially on the Continent, the swollen fibres are fixed by treating the hides with a weak solution of formaldehyde, which also acts as a preliminary tanning agent. The tannage can then be rapidly completed with fairly strong extracts, as the formaldehyde prevents the contraction of the grain which would ensue if untreated raw pelts were placed in strong tan liquor. The acid-formaldehyde process is risky, and cannot be recommended. The use of the artificial tannin, neradol, has replaced it in many Continental sole-leather tanneries. A preliminary tannage with neradol forms a good mordant for the use of the strong extracts.

FIG. 26
PINNING SOLE BUTTS

Whatever the method used to improve or depreciate the natural tannage, the surplus material left on the surface is raised or brushed off, and, after the leather has been left to drain for a few hours, it is sent to the finishing department, which is usually the drying shed. There, it is left piled up for a day or two, until it is in the right condition for oiling. The leather must be oiled, otherwise the grain would be harsh and brittle when dry, and would darken in colour, especially at the edges. Cod oil is generally used, and sometimes a little mineral oil is added to it to prevent possible impurities in the fish oil rising to the surface of the leather or causing damage in other ways. A cod oil purified by distillation would, however, be quite safe to use, and there seems to be no reason why tanners should use crude oils so frequently as they do, now that a large number of oils specially prepared for the leather trade are available. Linseed oil is also used in admixture with cod oil, its oxidising properties hastening the process of drying. The leather is liberally oiled with a brush or swab on the grain side and immediately hung up in the drying shed, where it is left until it reaches what is technically known as a "sammed" condition (*i.e.*, just damp enough to exude no water when the leather is doubled over). It is then struck out ("pinned") on the grain side, either with a hand tool (Fig. 26) or by machine. In the former case, the leather is placed on a long wooden beam and the pinner works from the left side, keeping two of the three edges of his knife flat on the leather while making heavy forward strokes. As the scum is worked out, the operator mops it up with a wet cloth. Machinery has replaced hand labour in this operation in all modern tanneries. The pressure of the tool removes scud and dirt, varying in quantity according to the amount of "bloom" contained in the particular tanning materials used. The leather is then laid in pile for a few hours, when it is in a fit condition for the first rolling, which is known in the trade as "rolling on." This operation is generally done by machine (Fig. 27) nowadays, but the old method of using a hand roller heavily weighted with an iron box (Fig. 28) is still practised in a few yards. After rolling, the leather is hung up again until nearly dry, when it is taken down and sized with a weak colouring matter, made up of annatto or tumeric, with chalk or whitening dissolved in white vinegar (acetic acid) and diluted. It is then rolled again ("rolling off") and polished with a piece of flannel. Finally, it is hung up to air off, and is then ready for the warehouse.

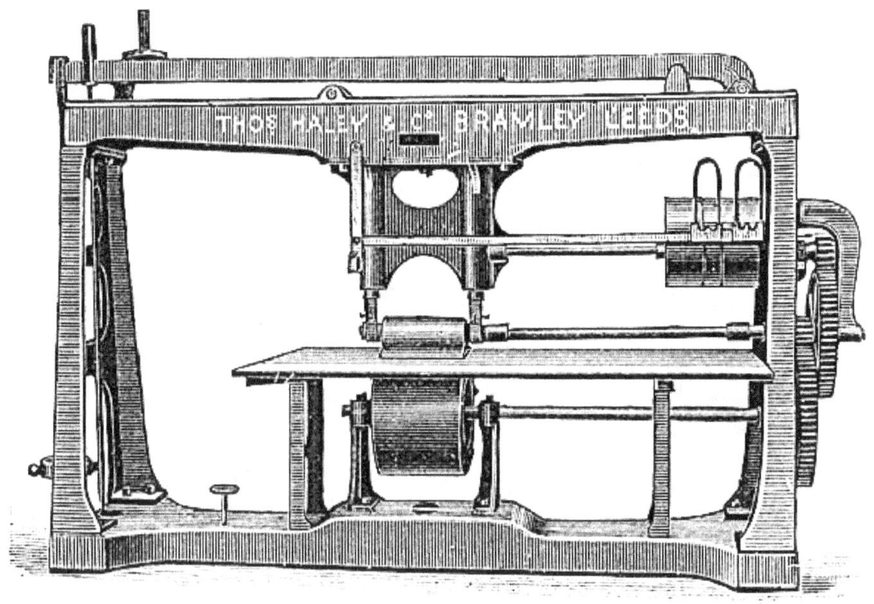

FIG. 27

ROLLING MACHINE

In many yards the finishing consists merely in striking out the leather, rolling it when properly tempered, hanging up until nearly dry, and re-rolling. An American machine for giving the final polish to sole leather has lately been introduced.

Instead of the rolling machine, some French tanners use the hammering machine, which gives good results, but is necessarily slow and frightfully noisy in action. The steel hammer moves up and down with remarkable rapidity, but only a small area is covered by each blow.

OLD METHOD OF ROLLING SOLE LEATHER

The artificial drying of sole leather, or of any other kind, is a matter that needs careful attention, for it is obvious that great delay would occur, and a large amount of business would be lost, if tanners relied solely on the climatic conditions of the British Isles; in fact, the weather is so rarely fit for drying leather that every up-to-date tannery contains some artificial aids, the need for which has been more pressing since a large proportion of leather contains a surplus of tanning matter which is liable to oxidise in contact with strong light and air, thereby darkening the leather and making it brittle.

Among the satisfactory drying plants are those of Howard-Smith & Co., and the Sutcliffe Ventilating and Drying Co., Ltd. Both work on the theory of fanning a continuous current of hot air through the drying-room, so that the moisture evaporating from the leather is constantly drawn off while the apparatus is at work.

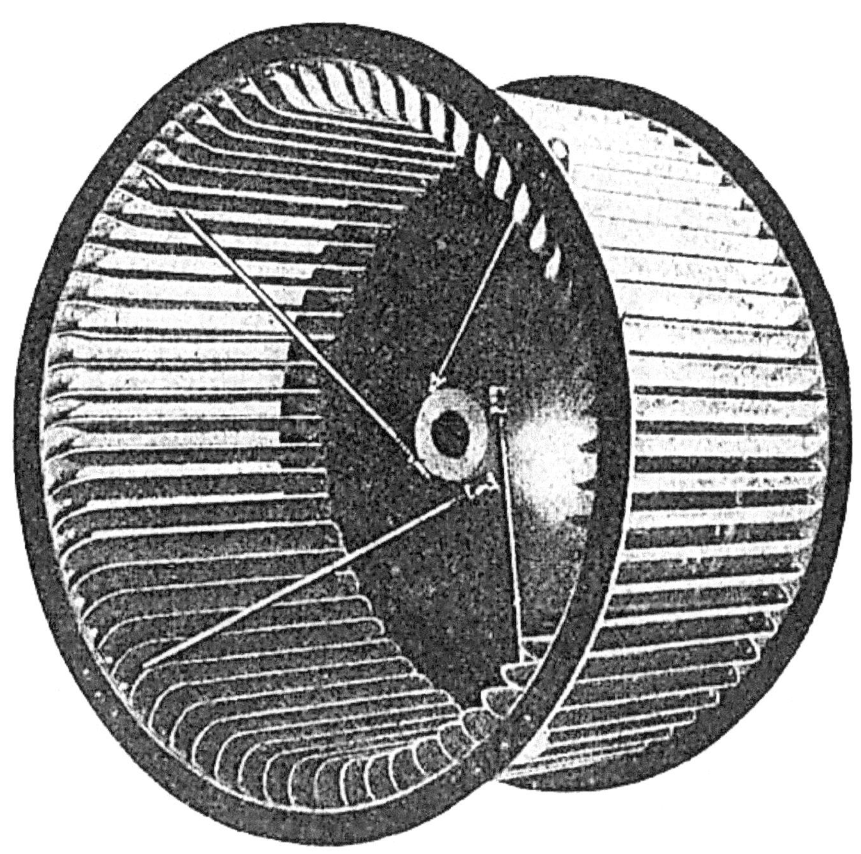

Fig. 29
FAN
(Howard-Smith system)

The Howard-Smith plant consists of a series of steel tubes into which hot water or steam is pumped. These pipes are enclosed in a chamber in which the air naturally acquires great heat. A fan (Fig. 29) is fixed in one side of this chamber (Fig. 30) and, when in motion, drives the hot air through a wide tube which leads to the drying chamber.

Figure 31 shows the Sutcliffe Fan and Heater installed in a tannery. At least two hygrometers should be hung up in a drying-room to determine the amount of moisture in the air.

Chrome Sole Leather

The manufacture of chrome sole leather suitable for ordinary walking boots is of comparatively recent origin, although natural chrome hides were dressed more than twenty years ago for tennis boot soles and other athletic shoes. There can be no doubt of the superior wearing and waterproof qualities of well-dressed chrome sole, but its high price, compared with that of vegetable-tanned sole leather, is against its general use.

Either the one bath or two bath tannage (described on p. 108) may be used, but, on the whole, the one bath method is preferred for the following reasons: (1) Its application is easier; (2) it produces a firmer and less elastic leather; and (3) there is practically no danger of weakening the hide fibres. On the other hand, the two-bath process produces a plumper leather which can, naturally, carry more dressing and command a correspondingly better price. In skilled hands, it is also under better control than the one-bath process, while it is absolutely necessary for the popular pale bluish-grey tint of chrome leather tennis soles.

FIG. 31
SUTCLIFFE SYSTEM OF DRYING

The natural chrome sole requires very little dressing. The chromed hides (usually rounded into butts or bends, shoulders and bellies) are allowed to remain on a horse two or three days after the completion of the tannage, so that the oxide of chromium may combine more firmly with the fibres. They are then placed in the drum tumbler again and washed in cold water for several hours. A constant stream is conveyed to the drum through a rubber pipe fixed to the tap, and escapes through small holes in the drum. The acid salts are not thoroughly removed by this washing and must, therefore, be neutralised with an alkali. Borax is the best for the purpose, owing to its mild action on leather and antiseptic properties. From 1 to 2 per cent. borax on the weight of the leather is generally sufficient, while, if soda be used for economical reasons, only half the quantity is required. The drum is revolved for about an hour; the liquor is then run off, and the leather receives a further washing in cold water for half an hour, when it is in a condition to receive the dressing, which is chiefly composed of materials which help to fill and lubricate the interstices of the fibres so that the substance is maintained and the natural strength of the fibres preserved. Gelatine, pure glue, Tragasol, paraffin wax, carnauba wax, spermaceti, Marseilles soap, are among the various ingredients used; while the delicacy of the tint may be improved with china clay or French chalk. Recipes vary considerably, each manufacturer claiming to have secret methods. Solutions are made of the ingredients, or, where one or more of the materials are insoluble, they are atomised in a mixing pan before use. To induce thorough penetration, the dressing liquid may be applied to the leather at a fairly high temperature, as chrome leather is unaffected by heat which would destroy the fibres of ordinary vegetable-tanned leather. Even so, it is inadvisable to use a higher temperature than 170° F. The leather is thoroughly impregnated with the dressing in about an hour's time, and is then piled on a wooden horse for several hours, or overnight, to drain and permit thorough incorporation of the dressing with the leather. When well-drained, the grain of the hides is smoothed by pressure with a special tool (Fig. 32) or by machine, the operation being known technically as "striking out." The machine (Fig. 34) gives quite satisfactory results and has replaced hand labour in all modern works. The hides are then "strained" (*i.e.*, extended and nailed to wooden frames), or they are simply hung up to dry. In the latter case, there is a small shrinkage of the size of the hide, but the substance is maintained. With good straining, a satisfactory increase of surface measurement can be obtained.

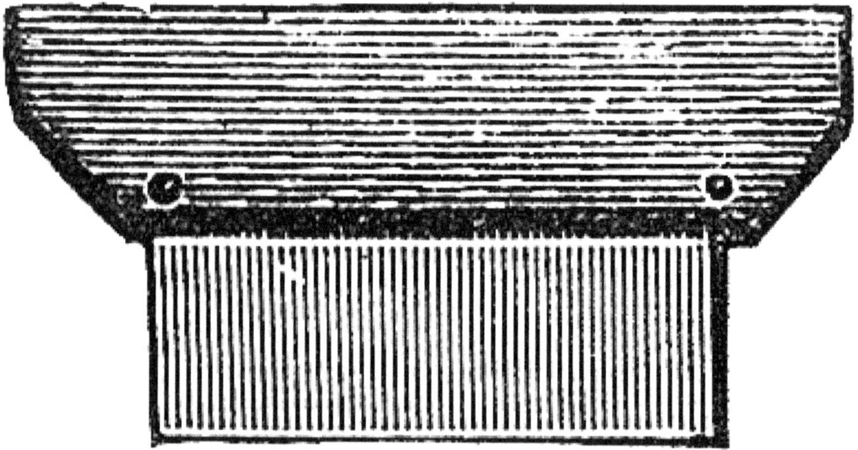

Fig. 32

SLEEKER

When the leather is completely dried, it may be sold at once, but if, as is generally the case, a special "nap" finish is required on the flesh side, the hides are placed in damped deal sawdust until they are in the right condition of flexibility for the next process, known as "fluffing." This is done on a rapidly revolving wheel (Fig. 33) covered with emery powder varying in the size of grain according to the effect desired on the finished leather. The abrasion of the leather on the flesh (*i.e.*, the under side) raises a soft nap. Carborundum, a special abrasive made in America, by the fusion of sand, coke, and salt at a very high temperature, has to some extent supplanted the use of emery. As a final finish, the flesh side may be rubbed over with chalk or china clay to give it a clear saleable appearance.

FIG. 33

FLUFFING MACHINE

The chrome sole leather used for ordinary boots is quite a different product, and it is only in the last two or three years that it has been used to any extent. The "Dri ped" is the best known make of this leather. The tannage is effected by the one or two-bath methods already described. The processes preparatory to chroming are very important, as it is essential to get the maximum yield of pelt. The hides are, therefore, often treated with sulphide of sodium, which loosens the hair in twenty-four hours or less. They are then placed in fairly strong limes for two or three days to swell the fibres and saponify the grease. After being washed in cold water, the hides are treated with a weak solution of lactic, boracic, or butyric acid, or butyrate of ammonia, to remove all trace of lime, when they are ready to be chrome-tanned. After chroming them, neutralisation of the acid chrome salts is effected with borax, and the leather is ready for dressing. The principal objects of this process are to make the leather firm and waterproof, and to remedy its tendency to slip easily on wet pavements. The last-named is the greatest difficulty, and there are only about two or three firms who have really surmounted it. Each manufacturer keeps his recipe secret, but the ingredients that go to make the various dressings are drawn from the following: Stearines, mineral oil, Tragasol, resin, carnauba wax, beeswax, paraffin wax, glue. Resin, or asphalt, or both, may be used to prevent the leather slipping in contact with a wet pavement. One patent describes a method of dressing chrome sole leather with a mixture of asphalt, resin, and paraffin wax.

Fig. 34

STRIKING-OUT AND SCOURING MACHINE

The waterproofing ingredients are preferably applied to the leather in the tumbler at a high temperature, say, 160-170° F. After running the drum for about three-quarters of an hour, the leather is impregnated with the mixture, and is then horsed up for at least twenty-four hours to allow complete incorporation of the fatty ingredients with the fibres of the leather. A suitable waterproof dressing and filling increases the strength of the leather.

The finishing of the leather is simple. The butts or bends are smoothed and stretched out by machine (Fig. 34), oiled on the grain, nailed or extended with special metal grips on square wooden frames, and dried. In some cases, they are hung up until nearly dry, rolled by machine instead of being put on boards and aired off in a drying stove.

A patented method of making waterproof chrome sole leather to prevent it slipping and losing its shape in wear consists in first treating the leather in a solution of glue, gelatine, agar-agar, or other colloidal substance, with the addition of formaldehyde, and then submitting it to strong pressure under the influence of a high temperature, in order to fix the colloidal matters. The pressure is made between heated plates. The leather is afterwards impregnated with a mixture of wool-grease, pitch, asphalt, resin, wax, gutta-percha, etc. A recipe given in the specification consists of wool grease (60 parts), asphalt (10 parts), soft pitch (25 parts) and gutta-percha (5 parts). The mass is fused and kept at 90° C. The hides are placed flat in this mixture, which they quickly absorb.

If the British Government should ever introduce a Bill to stop the adulteration of leather, it may be found somewhat difficult to deal with chrome sole, which must have some filling material to make its use practicable. No exception can be taken to the dressing of leather with materials that make it waterproof and increase its strength; in fact, much more will be done in this direction than has ever been attempted in the past, as waterproof sole leather is a necessity in Great Britain. Any measure to check the adulteration of leather must, therefore, clearly define the chemicals which are known to be harmful in leather and which may not be used. This has not been overlooked by the Australian Government, which has forbidden the use of barium salts in leather, and likewise the importation of leather boots or any goods made of leather containing this chemical. Such goods sent to Australia are liable to confiscation, and it is reported that a few consignments of boots have already been condemned.

Leather, either exported or imported, must not contain more than 3 per cent. of glucose unless the percentage is marked on each consignment, in which case, it is presumed, a tanner may use as much of the adulterant as he likes, although the fact that he has to disclose this practice acts as a deterrent in most cases. Unfortunately, the Australian Act leaves an important loophole, since the use of Epsom salts, which can be made to increase the weight of leather more than any other chemical, is not prohibited. In any case, none of these hygroscopic materials is of any use to chrome sole, for they would attract moisture which it is desirable to resist.

Vache Sole Leather

As its name implies, vache sole leather is a Continental product, being made chiefly in France, Belgium, and Germany. The raw material consists of light and medium cow hides. The details of working are somewhat similar to those used in tanning English sole leather, the main difference being that the hides are suspended in the lime liquors instead of throwing them in flat. The system of tannage is not so varied as the English, since the materials used generally consist of oak and pine barks, myrobalans, quebracho and oak extracts; and the finishing materials are of quite another character. The Continental tanners generally use the Réaumur thermometer, while the Beaumé hydrometer is used to determine the density of the tan liquors in place of the English barkometer (Fig. 24). One degree Beaumé is equal to 6.9° barkometer.

Vache leather is more pliable than English sole leather, but the addition of valonia extract towards the end of the tanning process would greatly increase its firmness.

The finish is applied to the flesh side of the leather, and a typical recipe consists of a size such as Irish moss or Tragasol (1 part), flour (20 parts), china clay (20 parts), and pure gambier (2 parts) in 200 parts of water. The size is dissolved and cooled, and the other ingredients are then added.

Machine Belting, Harness, and Saddlery Leathers

These leathers are rarely made by one firm; usually, strap butts and most kinds of belting leathers are dressed by curriers, whose trade is quite distinct from that of currying shoe leather. The tanning and currying of harness and saddlery leathers is another special branch. Besides these three important trades, there is the dressing of hydraulic, mechanical, and other industrial leathers, which likewise form special sections of the heavy leather industry.

Belting leather is an important item in the trade, and, as a good proportion is made from the finest hides, this class of leather is among the most expensive made. At present, there is much controversy in the trade as to whether the vegetable-tanned or the chrome-tanned article is the more economical in use. Briefly, chrome belting is superior in works where there is much steam or mineral acids, as it is not affected by these conditions to the same extent as bark-tanned belting. Its tensile strength is also greater, but against these advantages must be set its higher cost and tendency to stretch unduly in comparison with the vegetable-tanned product. It can be safely said, however, that the use of chrome belting is on the increase, although its production is not nearly on such a big scale as that of the old type of belting.

The tannage of belting leather is similar to that of sole leather, except that there is no necessity to continue the process, after the tannin has struck through, with the object of increasing its firmness and weight. Attention must also be paid to the class of tanning materials used, especially for belting of the best quality, as it must have great tensile strength and stand a severe strain in the dynamometric test. Tannins that rapidly oxidise in contact with light and air have, therefore, to be avoided. The oak bark tannage, with a little chestnut and oakwood extracts to finish the process, is a good method of imparting to the hide the right degree of firmness and flexibility.

As in the case of sole leather, belting may be artificially weighted during the tannage, although it is usually done in the currying process, if at all. There can be no doubt that a quantity of adulterated belting leather is made, and will continue to be made while the practice of selling by weight is in vogue. As a rule, sophisticated belting leather has a much weaker tensile strength than the pure product and is of relatively poor value, since the reduction of price is usually a matter of only a few pence. If users of belting bought on the principle of value instead of price, they would never buy adulterated leather.

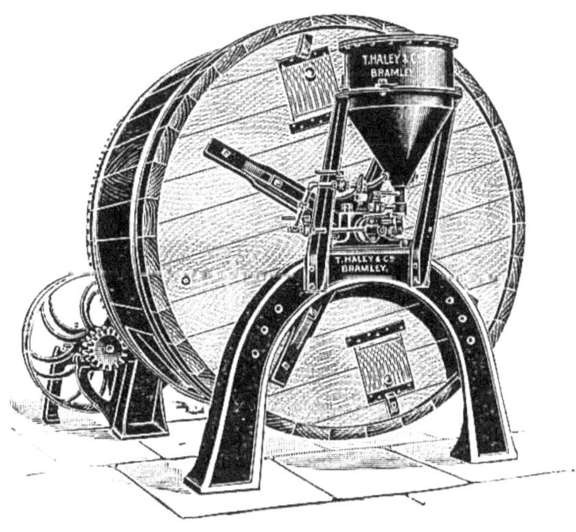

Fig. 35
LEATHER-STUFFING DRUM

In tanning hides for belting, the shoulders and bellies are cut off and usually dressed for sole or harness leather, leaving the butt, the prime part of the hide, 4-1/2 ft. in length (Fig. 23). The tanned butt is first shaved to level the substance, then washed in a solution of borax, and sumached in the drum. After smoothing the leather in the striking-out machine, it is partially dried ("sammed") and then rubbed on both sides with a dubbin of cod oil and tallow. In this condition the butts are left piled up for a few days, so that the dubbin penetrates the leather, which is then extended with the sleeker (Fig. 32) to make it smooth and to remove surplus grease, which is sold to soap-makers under the currier's name of "moisings." The leather is finally dried, rolled (optional), stretched by machine, and cut up in the width of belting required. Instead of "hand-stuffing" the leather with cod oil and tallow, which is still the best method, a large quantity of butts are now "drum-stuffed," the object being to make use of stearines, which are harder and heavier greases than tallow. The type of drum shown in Figure 35, in which the grease is incorporated with the leather by means of live steam, gives satisfactory results, although hot air apparatus is now replacing the steam injector.

A patent has lately been granted to an American inventor for the production of a strong and cheap belting. Flesh splits of hides are simply stuck together with a collodion or nitrocellulose solution. Any number of layers may be used, according to the substance required, the only essential quality being that the leather should be free from grease. The adhesive property of nitrocellulose solutions is probably stronger than that of any other material, but, unfortunately, the tough film they form on drying does not grip a greasy surface. Before the solution used to join the pieces of leather together is dry, the leather is rolled under heavy pressure, and, when thoroughly dried, can be cut up for belting.

The dressing of harness leather is similar to the manual process of making belting, with the exception that the butts or bends (half butts) are stained either black or a pale straw colour, the latter being known to the trade as the "London colour." Annatto is often used to get this colour. The bright, greasy finish on harness leather is obtained by rubbing buck tallow over the grain and polishing with a glass sleeker or a piece of flannel. The operation is sometimes done by machine, in which the working cylinder is covered with pieces of cotton rag.

Saddlery leathers are dressed on similar lines, but the finish is not so greasy as harness. Pig skins make the best and toughest leather for this purpose. They are dressed in a similar manner to harness hides, but special attention has to be given to pig skins to get rid of the large quantity of natural grease they contain.

Boot Upper Leathers

Whereas the number of different kinds of boot upper leathers in use less than three decades ago was limited to five or six (waxed calf, calf kid, French kid, mock kid, levant, coloured calf) it is now almost legion. Although the variety is almost bewildering, however, the popular demand is confined to about half-a-dozen sorts, which include real and imitation box calf, box hide, *glacé* or glazed kid, patent leather, willow calf, dull-finished chrome leather, and waxed kip butts and waxed splits for workmen's boots.

Box leathers and glazed kid are the most popular of all. Generally speaking, glazed kid is more suitable for wear in the summer and autumn; while box leather, being thicker and stronger, is preferable for the winter. Imitation willow calf (*i.e.*, calf skin tanned in vegetable and chrome liquors, either separately or combined) is very suitable for easy-wearing boots, but is not so durable and resistant to water as the pure chrome-tanned article.

The tannage of box and willow leathers may be effected by the one or two-bath process already described (p. 108). Before the tannage, it is advisable to pickle the hides or skins in a solution of alum and salt, with the object of preventing contraction of the tissues of the hide, and providing a mordant for the more rapid absorption and fixation of the chrome salts. The tannage completed, the acid salts in the leathers are neutralised with borax, and after the leather has been washed in warm water it is ready for dyeing. The dyeing of box calf is generally done in the drum tumbler, but there are several other methods. One system used on the Continent is to dip the skins, a pair at a time and placed flesh to flesh, in a very strong dye liquor. This method is slow, and not in accordance with modern ideas; used for producing browns and fancy shades, it is very difficult to avoid irregularity of colour where large parcels are manipulated. Another method is vat dyeing, the process being carried out in a wooden vat (Fig. 25) and the dye liquor circulated by means of a paddle. The one advantage of this system is that the leather can be easily examined during the process. A useful method of dyeing is carried out by brushing the colouring materials on the grain side of the leather. This process is economical, and it has the further advantage that the finished leather can be used for unlined boots and other purposes where an undyed flesh is necessary.

The original "box" leather was dyed a dark-blue shade in the drum before it was shaved, and, as the dye does not penetrate very far into chrome leather, unless a strong mordant of tannin be previously used, the subsequent shaving left the flesh side of the leather a very pale-bluish tint.

The process of dyeing is least troublesome and most effective when done in the drum tumbler. The leather is run in warm water until the temperature reaches 140°-150° F (60°-66° C.) and the dyeing materials are added gradually in a box at the side of the drum whence it passes through the axle or journal into the tumbler. Although chrome leather is not materially affected by boiling water in contradistinction to vegetable-tanned leather, which cannot be treated with water above 60° C. without injury, it is inadvisable to dye it in boiling solutions, the above-mentioned temperature being the most satisfactory. There are two methods of dyeing blacks in the leather trade: (1) the logwood-ammonia, and (2) the aniline black. The former is the cheaper of the two and quite satisfactory, although many dyers seem to prefer the aniline process. The latter certainly gives a deeper black, but it is not at all necessary to make the flesh side of box calf black, and many buyers prefer the back blue, although, of course, the grain side of the leather must be finished a jet black. The crude logwood is generally subjected to a process of fermentation or "ageing." The new wood has to be placed on stone or cemented flooring in a warm room and frequently turned over until fermentation has ceased, which usually takes about a week. It is then cut into small chips by machinery and packed in bags. This is the form in which it always used to enter the tannery, but it is now generally prepared in paste or crystal extract by makers of tanning and dye-wood extracts, a business which grows in importance every year. The colouring matter of logwood is haematoxylin, which is converted into haematin by oxidation; hence, the extract is often referred to as haematin crystals. The paste may be used where it is desirable to increase the substance of the leather, but most dyers prefer the crystals, which are easily dissolved in hot water. One lb. of crystals, to which is added just enough ammonia to change the brown colour to violet blue, suffices for each 100 lb. of leather dyed. The colouring matter is absorbed by the time the drum has been running half an hour, leaving clear water behind. The next process is known technically as "fat-liquoring," which, as its name implies, consists in lubricating the fibres of the leather with fatty or oily matters. This is a very important process, for, when suitable ingredients are used, the pliability, strength, and waterproof quality of the leather are greatly increased. The making of special fat-liquors for different kinds of leather has become quite an important business, and most makes can be depended upon for the specified purposes. It is a debatable point as to whether fat-liquoring should precede or follow dyeing. Generally speaking, it is better to adopt the latter course, as the fatty ingredients help to fix the colouring matter on the fibres of the leather. The dye is also less liable to fade when fat liquoring follows the colouring.

The number of materials that may be used for the process of fat-liquoring is almost legion, but the principal are soaps, oils, egg-yolk, tallow, flour, Tragasol, Irish moss, china clay, and starch. Unless the special preparations made by leather trade chemical firms be used, much care has to be exercised in selecting the most suitable ingredients for each class of leather. For example, the mixture that would give good results on vegetable-tanned leather might be quite unsuitable for chrome leather. Then, again, the selection of material is based on the style of finish required, a dull finish necessitating heavy fats and greases which would be quite unsuitable for bright leathers, and particularly for those of the chrome-tannage. Among the hundreds of recipes that have been published from time to time, tallow has only found a place in one or two mixtures, yet it is one of the finest materials for strengthening and lubricating the fibres of leather. If its splendid properties were fully known, it would be very largely used for fat-liquoring purposes. Of course, it is well known to the currying trade, having for several centuries formed the basis, together with cod oil, of the dubbin used in stuffing waxed leather and belting butts.

The following is a useful recipe for a fat-liquor for box calf: 2 lb. Marseilles soap and 3 lb. neatsfoot oil for every 100 lb. of leather. The soap is cut into small pieces and dissolved in hot water, and the oil is added slowly and thoroughly mixed by stirring vigorously. Where possible, emulsification should be done in a machine, in order to atomise the ingredients. The finer they can be brought into a state of division, the better they will be absorbed by the leather. Other suitable fat-liquors for box leathers are the following: (1) Turkey red oil, 2 per cent. of weight of leather and neutral soap 1 per cent.: (2) neatsfoot oil, 2 lb.; tallow, 1 lb.; and Tragasol, 1 lb.: (3) cod oil, 2 lbs.; Marseilles soap, 1 lb.: (4) neatsfoot oil, 2 lbs.; egg-yolk, 1/2 lb., or six fresh yolks. The process is completed in 20-30 minutes.

In the case of fancy colours or browns, the leather should generally be well-drained and warmed up again in the drum in hot water (170° F.) before fat-liquoring, but the precaution is unnecessary for black leathers. After the fat-liquoring process, the leather is removed from the drum, and piled up on the horse to drain, and left for several hours or overnight, to allow it to assimilate the fatty ingredients. It is then submitted to an operation known as sleeking or striking out, with the object of removing surplus water and so facilitating drying, and making the grain side smooth. Machinery is now almost universally employed, especially for chrome leather. A good type of striking out machine is shown in Figure 34.

If done by hand, the skins are placed on a sloping glass or slate table, with the flesh side uppermost, which is then stretched out by strong pressure with a tool known as a sleeker, the strokes being made downward in the direction of the hair growth. The flesh side done, the whole skin is turned over and the grain side is similarly treated. Sometimes only the flesh side is struck out, especially if the grain is soft and tender. The sleeker consists of an iron, steel, or copper blade, about 6 in. square, fitted in a wood handle (Fig. 32). The skins are hung up in the drying-room immediately they are extended and smoothed by sleeking, and are then either allowed to dry completely, or, as is generally the case with best leather, they are hung up until a great deal of the moisture is evaporated and the skins are left in a slightly moist, or, as it is generally termed, "sammed" condition. The skins are then taken down, damped in dry parts, folded over, laid in piles to equalise the moisture, and finally smoothed out and stretched again by hand or machine. This second operation after the dyeing is known as "setting."

Chrome-tanned skins are usually stretched and nailed on square boards after setting, as, owing to their elasticity, they are liable to shrink considerably in drying. The superficial area can be increased by fully extending the skins. This operation is technically described as "straining." It may be stated here that vegetable-tanned leathers are not generally "strained" on boards, as such leather is better in quality and substance when hung up and dried. Leather of combined tannage (*i.e.*, tanned with vegetable and chrome products) is, however, frequently "strained," as the astringent property of chrome would otherwise cause contraction of the fibres.

When dried on the boards the leather is somewhat stiff, and has, therefore, to be softened before any finishing ingredients are applied. Chrome leather is softened by placing it for a few days in damp sawdust, which, for brown or fancy coloured leather, must be of deal or white pine, and, therefore, free from objectionable colouring matter; but, for black leather, the sawdust of any wood is suitable. The skins must be systematically piled one above the other, and a little damped sawdust scattered over each skin.

When properly "seasoned," the skins are brushed free of the sawdust and "staked," either by hand or machine, usually by the latter means. The staking knife may be fixed in a wood crutch (arm stake), or fixed upright in a vertical wooden stand (knee stake). In the former case, the skins to be staked must be secured in a horizontal wooden groove fixed to two uprights, the workman then pressing heavily in a downward direction with the staking knife, of which the crutch is held under the armpit. In using the upright stake, the leather is moved to and fro over the edge of the fixed knife. Both of these manual operations are arduous and somewhat dangerous, and should be displaced by machinery wherever possible (Fig. 36).

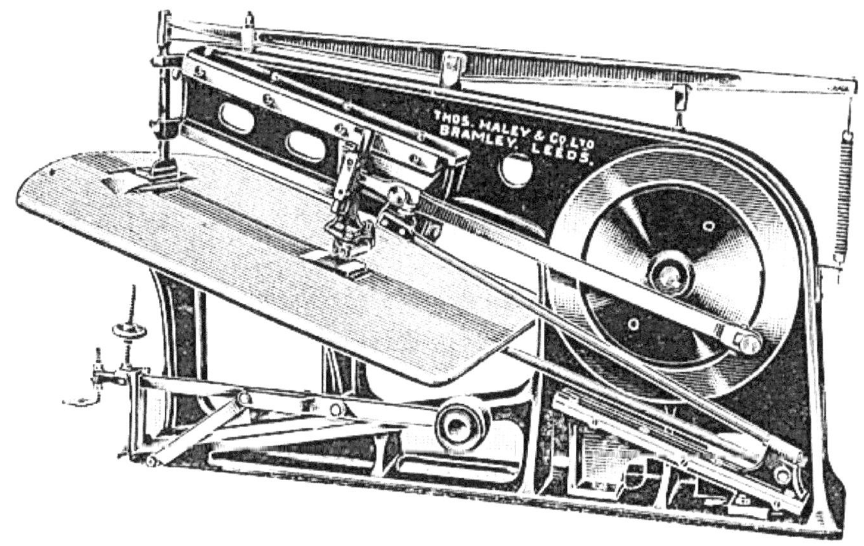

Fig. 36

STAKING AND GLAZING MACHINE

The thoroughly softened leather is then dried, mordanted with a solution of logwood, or haematin crystals, blacked with levant ink, a specially prepared black dye, or with a suitable aniline dye, and dried again. It is finally seasoned with a glutinous or albuminous mixture (blood albumen, milk, and a little aniline black dye make a good mixture), dried, glazed, seasoned a second time, and reglazed. A light coating of mineral oil turns the finish into a jet black, and the leather is ready for the warehouse. There are several types of glazing machines, but the "grasshopper" (so called owing to its action) is the most popular for box calf. This machine is the same as shown in Figure 36, except that the working tool is replaced with a smooth glass or agate roller.

The term "box" applied to this leather was invented by a prominent American tanner, and had he registered the name and patented his process he would have reaped a very rich harvest, for the leather is used in enormous quantities throughout the world. As it was, the American firm tried to obtain an injunction against English firms manufacturing the leather, but had to withdraw their claim, as they were not the inventors of chrome leather, which was made in Scotland before it was introduced to the States. Moreover, the word "box," as applied to leather, was not registered in the United Kingdom.

Willow calf is exactly the same kind of leather as box calf, except that it is dyed brown instead of black. The seasoning mixture naturally differs and may consist of a mixture of egg albumen, milk, and a little of the same, or similar, dye solution as that used in the dyeing process. In order to get clear colouring, the dyes should be well dissolved and strained through fine muslin.

Chamois Leather

This kind of leather is well known to the general public under the name of wash-leather, but it is, perhaps, not so widely known that there is practically no real chamois leather available, since the species of animal bearing this name is almost extinct. Nowadays, "chamois," or "shamoy" is made from the flesh split of sheep skin, and the method whereby the leather is produced is described as the oil tannage. The chamois leather dresser may also do the preliminary work of fellmongering, but more often he receives the pelts, or "fells," from the fellmonger. Although the pelts have been in a lime liquor known as the fellmonger's "gathering limes," the process of liming has to be continued and carefully regulated. Too much liming makes the pelts loose, owing to the development of bacteria. This effect would cause the finished leather to be soft and spongy. On the other hand, under-liming fails to remove sufficient of the cement substance which binds the fibres of the pelts; consequently, the leather produced from these pelts is thin and somewhat gristly. After being limed, the skins are "cobbed" (*i.e.*, the bits of wool or hair left on by the fellmonger are removed) and the pelts are then fleshed by machinery. The next operation, splitting, is very important and requires skilful attention to get good results. The Reeder machine is largely in use, but the band-knife machine is also suitable. The top half of the sheep skin (*i.e.*, the grain side) is utilised for the manufacture of skivers, while the under portion, or flesh side, technically called "lining," serves as the raw material for chamois leather. The best linings are generally sorted out for making into parchment, which, of course, commands a much higher price than chamois. Linings for chamois are then submitted to the operation of either re-splitting or frizing, the object being to remove the loose tissue lying between the grain and flesh. The pelts are re-split in the case of cheap chamois, but frized if intended for choice finish. Frizing is an operation peculiar to the making of chamois and glove leather. It is done with a very sharp knife, similar to the fleshing knife, and on a more upright beam than that used by tanners. The work requires great skill, frizers being among the best paid workers in the trade. Frizing done, the linings are freed from lime by washing them in the drum tumbler, or paddle-vat, through which cold water is allowed to flow continuously for two or three hours. When lamb skins, which are too thin to split, are made into chamois leather, the grain is removed by frizing.

A quick and effective method of deliming is to treat the skins in a weak solution of lactic acid. Some dressers use a drench of pea-flour or bran. The mild acids produced by the fermentation of these materials not only neutralise the lime but also reduce the gristly nature of the skins to a soft, supple condition. The bran infusion is slightly warmed to hasten the process of fermentation, but the temperature must not exceed 100° F. (32° C.). The linings are then rinsed in cold water and sent to the stocking machines, in which they are kneaded until they become quite soft. Either the faller-stocks or the mechanical pushers (Fig. 14) may be used, the latter being the more modern machine. The operation may require from four to ten hours, the completion being determined by the condition of the skins. "Samming" follows stocking, and for this purpose the linings are hung up in the drying shed until thoroughly dripped, but not dried. In this slightly damp condition they are then prepared for the next process of oiling, which is the most important part of chamois-dressing, as it converts the perishable raw linings into leather. In the United Kingdom, cod oil (generally Newfoundland) is used exclusively, and gives best results. Whale and shark liver, or menhaden oils are often used abroad.

The linings are placed in a tub or vat, a few at a time, and oil is poured over each layer until a sufficient number has been treated to fill the stocking machine. The stocks are run for half-an-hour, or until the oil has penetrated the linings, when they are put back into the vat, where they remain for about an hour. They are then re-stocked, taken into the shed to samm, re-oiled in the vat, and stocked again. These processes are repeated until the skins are thoroughly impregnated with the oil, when they are dried in a warm stove. The skins are not yet converted into leather, which only occurs in oil-dressing, after the oxidation of the oil. This is effected by spontaneous heat, the dry oiled skins being heaped in boxes and covered. Strict attention has to be paid to avoid over-heating the skins, which are turned over and changed at intervals. When the leather ceases to heat, the process is completed. It is then dipped into hot water and mechanically pressed, to remove surplus or uncombined oil, which is collected and sold under the name of "sod oil." The leather is afterwards drummed in warm water and finely cleansed in an alkaline solution, potash, soda, or borax, chiefly the first named, being used for this purpose. They are then rinsed in water, dried, damped, and softened by staking. At this stage, the best skins are sorted out for the glove makers. The others are finished for wash-leather by re-staking, paring with the moon-knife, and smoothing both sides of the skin with a scurfer, or fine pumice-stone. In the warehouse, they are damped, stretched out, piled up, and kept fully extended by placing heavy weights near the edges of each pile of skins.

Gloving Leather

Progress in the art of making leather for gloves has been rapid during the last few years; but further important developments are expected, particularly in the process of tanning. Practically the only method that has been used for many decades for converting kid, lamb, and sheep skins into gloving leather is that known technically as "tawing," which consists of treating skins with alum, salt, egg-yolk, flour, and a vegetable oil. These substances change skins into extremely supple and "stretchy" leather, but when this is made into gloves it is far from ideal in wear, because it fails to keep the hands warm in cold, wet weather, it is easily soiled and cannot be cleaned without great expense, and it is not very strong in texture. Combination tannages have lately been produced, however, which remove the defects of alumed leather. By means of a light chrome tannage after tawing, the leather is strengthened and made more resistant to water, and can be cleaned with a damp rag or sponge. By tanning skins with the formaldehyde process, or with Neradol, the artificial tannin, for making into suède leather, the finished article is not only washable but also resists the action of alkalies and soap. The adaptation of combined tannages in the manufacture of gloving leathers has only lately been developed, and further improvements will doubtless be effected before long.

Lamb, kid, goat, and sheep skins constitute the raw material for gloving leathers, although deer and antelope skins are also used to a small extent. Real kid skins are the best wearing dress gloves, but the great majority of so-called "kid" gloves are made of lamb skins. The raw kid and lamb skins are chiefly of European, Arabian, and Indian origin. Sheep skins from the Cape provide the raw material for a large number of men's gloves, and leather of very good quality can be produced from the best grades. Most of the skins are preserved by drying, or by salting and drying, although some kid skins are wet-salted and packed in barrels for export. It would save leather-dressers a great deal of trouble if they could always get wet-salted skins; but the object of drying them is to reduce the weight and lower the cost of freight. Soaking is done by methods already described (p. 65). Loose flesh and pieces of fat are cut off in order to facilitate the action of the depilitant, of which the best for glove leather is undoubtedly a paste of lime and red arsenic. Seven or eight parts of lime to one of arsenic is a satisfactory proportion, the quantities to be mixed depending on the number of skins to be treated, as a fresh mixture should be made for each lot, or "pack" as the tanner terms it. The lime should be well broken up, or, better still, pure powdered lime should be used and the red arsenic well mixed with it; a little water is then added to slake the lime gradually, and the mixture is stirred to promote chemical reaction. The compound is further diluted with water until it has the right consistency and the colour has changed. The reaction generates great heat, and the "paint" should, therefore, not be used at once. The flesh side is mopped with the paint and the skins are folded flesh to flesh. After a few hours, or as soon as the hair or wool is loosened, the skins are dehaired or dewoolled. The hair or wool is not allowed to come into contact with the depilitant, otherwise it would be damaged. In large yards, the white hair is separated from the coloured, as it is worth nearly twice as much. Wool is sorted into different qualities, of which the number may vary from four to eight, or even nine, according to the class of skins treated. The pelts are then thoroughly washed and placed in lime liquors, where they remain for one or two weeks, being hauled and set in the usual manner. Fleshing and piecing or trimming are the next operations, and then follows the very important process of puering, which, in the case of glove leather, must be thoroughly done so as to reduce the pelts to a very soft and flaccid condition. Success in the making of glove leather depends largely on the "puering" process.

In most of the English tanneries a decoction of dog manure is used, at a temperature not exceeding 90° F., but on the Continent the artificial puer, oropon, is preferred. It is much safer to use and more uniform in its action than excrement, which develops bacteria rapidly in contact with gelatinous pelts, and could ultimately destroy them entirely. After puering them, the pelts are well washed and submitted to the process of drenching, which consists in putting the skins into a warm infusion of bran or pea-flour and leaving them covered until the following morning. The slightly acid fermentation causes the pelts to rise to the top of the vat. They are pushed into the liquor again with a pole and stirred round. This is repeated three or four times to prevent damage to the grain. The process is often done in the paddle-vat (Fig. 25), in which the bran liquor is circulated for several hours before the pelts are allowed to remain quiescent. Drenching thoroughly purges the pelts of the last traces of lime, and puts them in suitable condition for being made into leather. The pelts are then rinsed in tepid water and "scudded" on the grain with a slate or vulcanite tool, shaped somewhat like a dehairing knife. The scud removed consists of dirt, dissolved lime salts, short hairs, and pigment. Machines are rapidly replacing manual labour for this operation.

The alum tannage, known technically as "tawing," is largely used for kid and lamb gloves. The tawing mixture is composed of alum, salt, egg-yolk, and wheaten flour. The proportions used vary considerably in different tanneries, but the following is a typical recipe: 4 lb. alum, 2 lb. salt, 1 lb. salted egg-yolk, or the yolks of twenty fresh eggs, and 5 lb. flour for 100 lb. of pelts. The flour is made into a paste, the egg yolk is diluted in warm water and mixed with the flour, the salt and alum are dissolved and added, and the mixture thoroughly stirred. A suitable quantity of water (about 2 gals. per 100 lb. pelts) is then placed in the drum tumbler, the tawing mixture is added, and the drum revolved for a few minutes before putting the pelts in. The process is completed in two or three hours in the case of thin skins. It is a good plan, however, to leave them at rest in the drum for a day, after which they are piled up overnight to allow further combination of the tawing materials with the fibres of the pelts. The leather is then dried out completely, damped in clean sawdust, or by sprinkling with water, levelled by shaving if necessary, staked over an upright knife fixed in a wooden stand or by machine, and dried in a hot stove. In this condition, or in the "crust," as dressers term it, the leather is allowed to remain several weeks to "age," a most essential process for the production of soft, and supple glove leather.

Dressing and dyeing are begun as soon as the leather is satisfactorily aged. The skins are uniformly soaked in warm water, dyed, and re-dressed with egg yolk ("re-egged"), to which a small quantity of olive oil, or a sulphonated oil, is added. Some dressers prefer to give the second tawing mixture before dyeing, but the advantage of dressing the leather after dyeing is that the colour is securely fixed. In "re-egging," many dressers use a similar mixture to the first dressing. The dyeing process is of great importance, since the colour must be fast. The leather is dyed either in the drum or on a convex table. In the former case, the leather is naturally coloured both sides, while, in the latter, it is stained with a brush on the grain side only. Staining is the more difficult method. Kid glove leather may be dyed with aniline colours, or, as more generally practised, with natural dye-woods as a base and aniline dye for top-colouring. The great advantages of the latter method are economy in dye-stuffs and increased depth of colour. The skins are first prepared for dyeing by brushing with, or drumming them in, an alkaline solution. Stale urine was largely used for this process, but ammonical salts are now generally preferred, if only for sanitary reasons. The skins are then drummed or paddled in, or brushed with, dye-wood liquids which have been carefully strained. A large selection is available, including fustic, cuba wood, saffron, peachwood, logwood, sappan wood, cutch, Persian berries, gambier or terra japonica, and golden tan bark.

Light and medium brown can be obtained from these dye-woods without the aid of aniline colours; but for dark shades, and to increase the brilliancy of other colours, a top dye or coal-tar dye is often given.

The natural dyes are further developed with "strikers," which mainly consist of metallic salts. Iron, copper, and zinc sulphates, nitrate and acetate of iron, bichromate of potash, and titanium salts (titanium lactate, titanium potassium oxalate, and tanno-titanium oxalate) are the most important. The lactate, sold commercially under the name of "corichrome," is especially suitable, as, unlike the mineral acid salts, especially the sulphates, it has no destructive effect on the fibres of the leather.

Dye-woods are now concentrated in the form of a paste, or dry extract, the latter being the more reliable. They are also very convenient to use and dissolve, while mixtures are, of course, easily prepared. A good tan shade on Cape sheep can be obtained by mordanting the leather with a solution of 1 lb. of bichromate of potash for every 100 lb. of leather, drumming it in 8-9 lb. of pure gambier, and then with a mixture of cuba wood extract, 1 lb.; fustic extract, 3/4 lb.; Brazil wood extract, 1/2 lb.; and logwood extract, 1/2 oz. After drumming the leather in this dye liquor for about an hour, the colour is developed with corichrome. If a darker shade be required, the leather can be treated with a suitable basic dye. After dyeing the leather, some dressers only fat-liquor it with egg-yolk and a small quantity of olive oil, while others prefer to re-dress it with a similar mixture to that used for tawing, namely, alum, salt, egg-yolk, and flour; but, where titanium salts are used, the latter method is not essential, because titanium has tanning properties. When dry, the leather is ready for finishing, but it is advisable to keep it in store for a few days before packing it in damp sawdust or sprinkling it with water to prepare it for the operation of staking. Anything more unlike leather would be difficult to imagine at this stage, but, after stretching the skin in the staking machine, or by drawing it over the upright stake, the dry, stiff, and shrivelled leather is reduced to a very supple condition. The flesh side of the leather is then pared with the moon-knife, or in the shaving machine, to equalise the thickness. In some works, a special tool which pares the leather on a flat table is preferred; this particular operation is called "doling." The flesh side is finished by fluffing it on the emery or carborundum wheel (Fig. 33). Finally, the grain is brushed and polished with the glass sleeker, or ironed.

Chamois leather has been largely used for gloves of late years, but this leather has the defect, in common with suède leathers, of getting soiled much more quickly than grain leathers, such as kid, lamb, or Cape sheep. Nevertheless, suède and chamois gloves are likely to remain fashionable to a more or less extent. The manufacture of chamois leather is described on page 144. Sun-bleached skins are the best for dyeing, especially if delicate shades are wanted. The frontispiece shows a field covered with skins bleaching in the sun. Chemically bleached leather is likely to become discoloured after dyeing. Defective skins are often dyed with pigments (dust colours), and this system is also applied to skins which have to be dyed such delicate shades as cannot be produced by wood or aniline colours. Although it gives attractive results to the eye, and certainly covers up any defects of the grain, this method of dyeing is not altogether satisfactory, as the leather remains unpleasantly dusty in wear for quite a long time.

The dyeing of chamois with wood-dyes or coal-tar colours is by no means easy, but this method gives the best results when successful. The grease must first be removed from the leather with a solution of 5 lb. of borax or 3-1/2 lb. of soda for every 100 lb. of leather. If the leather is still greasy on the surface, a further quantity of soda or borax is given, after which the leather is well washed in warm water, sumached, rinsed to remove the particles of sumach, and mordanted with titanium salts. The dyeing is then done with anilines or wood-dyes, or a combination of both, and this is followed by fat-liquoring with egg-yolk and a sulphonated oil. The finishing operations are staking and fluffing.

To get a good, fast black on chamois and suède leathers is one of the difficult processes in the leather trade, although it is easier to get a good black on alumed or chromed leather than on vegetable-tanned. Alumed leather is washed in a solution of borax or carbonate of ammonia to remove uncombined dressing in order to prepare it for dyeing. Chrome-tanned suède leather does not need this preparation. The leather is first mordanted with dye-wood extract, of which a suitable mixture is logwood and fustic, or logwood and quercitron, in the proportion of 4 lb. and 2 lb. to every 100 lb. of leather. After drumming the leather in this solution for about an hour, a weak solution of copperas (ferrous sulphate) and bluestone (copper sulphate) is added, and the milling is continued for twenty minutes, when the leather is well prepared to receive the black dye. Instead of the iron and copper salts, corichrome is often preferred, as it is quite safe to use, whereas iron salts have a destructive action on the fibres of the leather, unless the precaution be taken to mordant the skins with a good quantity of dye-wood extract.

Following the application of the iron or corichrome striker, the leather is dyed with suitable aniline black (leather black, or corvoline) and finally fat-liquored to nourish the leather, and to fix and intensify the black. This recipe also gives good results where the skins are dyed only on the flesh side, the solutions being applied with a brush.

White Washable Leather

Among the new kinds of leather for gloves, none is more remarkable or more useful than the washable sheep or goat skins. The great advantage of this leather is that it can be washed in warm water and soap any number of times without injury, whereas gloves of ordinary tawed kid and lamb skins have to be dry cleaned and cannot be renovated many times. An additional advantage of washable leather is its warmth. After being dehaired, puered and drenched, the skins are drummed in a solution of formaldehyde and soda. In two or three hours, the skins are tanned, and are then treated with a solution of sulphate of ammonia. The quantities required are about 3 lb. of formaldehyde (40 per cent.) and 8 lb. of sodium carbonate (80 per cent.), and 1 lb. of sulphate for 100 lb. of pelts, using sufficient water to cover the skins well in the drum. This tannage produces a white but somewhat thin and empty leather, and the fat-liquoring must, therefore, be filling and softening. An emulsion of white curd soap and olive oil, or of egg-yolk and neatsfoot oil, is suitable. "Crestanol," a special preparation, also gives satisfactory results, since it is adapted for giving nourishment and resiliency to thin, empty leather.

Fancy Leathers

The best known of the fancy leathers is "morocco." This variety has been made for ages, and the name probably originated from the fact that very fine leathers of this kind were manufactured in Morocco a few centuries ago. History records that a similar leather, dyed red, was made in the ninth century before the Christian era.

The best morocco leather is made from Continental goat skins, which are mostly obtained from Central Europe and Spain. The Norwegian goat skins are also said to be of good quality for the morocco finish. An inferior morocco leather, which is produced in large quantities, is manufactured from East India goat skins, while a cheaper grade still can be produced from certain classes of East India sheep skins. The real moroccos are tanned in sumach, but the cheaper sorts are tanned in India with babool or turwar bark and re-tanned in sumach in the countries to which they are exported, chiefly Great Britain, Germany, France, and America.

One of the best methods of sumach-tanning goat and calf skins is that known as the "bottle" tannage. Each skin is doubled over and sewn by machine round the edge, leaving part of the neck unsewn. The skins are then turned inside out and filled with a strong infusion of sumach, and floated in a tub containing sumach liquor. After being a few hours in the tub, the skins are heaped one above the other in a large pile, where the pressure forces the tannin through the skins. The process can be completed in twenty to twenty-four hours, after which the skins are cut open, rinsed, and finished in the usual manner. This method of tanning is now largely replaced by the use of paddle-vats (Fig. 25).

The dyeing and finishing are somewhat similar to that of coloured boot upper leather, except that the leather is slightly oiled on the grain instead of being fat-liquored. There are several different methods of graining morocco leather; some of the grains are made naturally by pressing the leather, when folded over, with a cork-covered board, while others are first embossed in various ways and then boarded. The well-known "crushed morocco" is produced by glazing the grained leather under heavy pressure.

Skivers, the grain splits of sheep skins (see p. 145) are extensively used for fancy articles. The majority are finished with a smooth grain for hat-bands, bookbinding, and linings. The grain of a sheep skin is, naturally, soft, and not very strong. To stiffen and strengthen the grain, an artificial layer, consisting of paste finishes, is often applied. Skins finished in this manner are termed "paste grain skivers." These are largely used for bookbinding and cheap purses. Sheep grains are sometimes given a finish somewhat similar to that of leather bags. This is produced in a printing machine by means of a copper roller which is run over the damp (but not too wet) leather. The skins are then described as "long-grain" skivers. The grain surface of sheep skins is particularly suitable for embossing, and wonderful imitations of all kinds of skins can be reproduced on skivers.

The fancy leather trade is not confined to these imitations, however, as real lizard, seal, ichneumon, alligators, crocodile, shark, porpoise, snake, and even frog skins (Japanese) are utilised.